A Coalville Miner's Story

SIXTY YEARS' RECOLLECTIONS OF WORK IN THE LEICESTERSHIRE COALFIELD

Maurice Woodward

ALAN SUTTON

LEICESTERSHIRE MUSEUMS, ARTS & RECORDS SERVICE

First published in the United Kingdom in 1993 by
Leicestershire Museums, Arts & Records Service

Managed by Alan Sutton Publishing Ltd
Phoenix Mill · Far Thrupp · Stroud · Gloucestershire

Leicestershire Museums, Arts & Records Service publication no. 125

British Library Cataloguing in Publication Data

A catalogue record for this book is available from the British
Library

ISBN 0–7509–0592–1

Typeset in 11/12 Garamond.
Typesetting and origination by
Alan Sutton Publishing Limited.
Printed in Great Britain by
Redwood Books, Trowbridge.

Contents

The Leicestershire Remembered series

General Editor: Steph Mastoris

Already published:

One man's Wigston: sixty years' recollections of everyday life
in Wigston Magna (1993)
O D Lucas

Foreword

This book is the second in a series by Leicestershire Museums, Arts & Records Service which publishes personal reminiscences by the people of Leicestershire and Rutland.

When so much of the work of Leicestershire Museums is directed at the preservation and interpretation of artefacts relating to everyday life in the county, it seems very fitting that the memories of the people who used such items are also recorded. Frequently, this has taken the form of recorded interviews, and the Service now has several hundreds of hours of taped conversations with many local people. A few museum publications have already drawn upon this material, perhaps the most notable being *Cap and Apron: an oral history of domestic service in the Shires, 1880-1950*, by Samuel Mullins and Gareth Griffiths (1986), and *Knitting Together*, by Siobhan Kirrane and Geoffrey Bowles (1990).

Often, however, people prefer to write down their memories and the success of the "As I Remember It" series produced by Leicestershire Libraries is a glowing testimony of this. The "Leicestershire Remembered" series aims to complement these small anthologies by publishing more lengthy accounts of life in the past which have a distinct bearing on the present.

The reminiscences that follow could not be more apt in fitting this brief, especially in the light of recent developments by Leicestershire Museums, Arts & Records Service in the Coalville area. On 27th June 1992 it opened the Snibston Discovery Park on the site of the former Snibston Colliery. From the beginning of this project the museum service staff were adamant that the human story of mining and all other Leicestershire industries should be the first priority, and the subsequent success of the Discovery Park has proved this to be a correct decision. Maurice Woodward's memoirs are central to this work because of their informed, yet human stance and we are most grateful to him for setting pen to paper and to Mr John Crocker for his great efforts in preparing the manuscript for publication.

Steph Mastoris and Stuart Warburton
Leicestershire Museums, Arts & Records Service

The author, Maurice Woodward, 1992.

Preface

Coal mining is a traditional industry of long standing in the district surrounding Coalville, a town established around the coal mines of Whitwick and Snibston in the early nineteenth century. With the closing of Bagworth Colliery in 1991 the last of the Leicestershire pits stopped production and a thousand year history of deep-mine coal extraction came to an end.

High quality coal seams which outcrop in the Coleorton area were among the first in the country to be exploited for fuel by ancient "bell-pit" techniques, and by the mid fifteenth century, a sophisticated industry had been established. One hundred years later the economic importance of their coal mines brought great prosperity to the Beaumonts of Coleorton Hall. As the shallow Main Seam was worked out, new coal mines followed the deeper resources as they dipped south-east towards the Thringstone Fault (see the sketch map on p. 9). By the early nineteenth century, accessible reserves around Coleorton and Swannington were nearing their end and the new foundations at Whitwick and Snibston drew away much of the mining community. To the south, Bagworth, Ellistown and other modern pits were opened and in the twentieth century New Lount Colliery was sunk on the Coleorton Estate. By this time the settlement of Coalville was well established and the mobile workforce largely travelled to work rather than relocate near the pits. Coalville thus became an important town at the centre of the Leicestershire coalfield.

Maurice Woodward, born and bred in a close-knit mining community, has spent all his working life down the pits. He is typical of the traditional coal miner in every way, except in his passion for writing. This little book is therefore of particular significance in giving a rare insight into the author's childhood and working experiences over a period of some 60 years, during which tremendous changes took place inside and outside this unattractive industry for which he was destined from the day he was born.

The dangers, conflicts and injustices imposed by a demanding regime are set against a background of poverty and frustrated hope. The war years are covered in a series of nostalgic cameos of life in the Home Guard, which provide some valuable historical accounts of this epoch and will bring back many memories to those who lived in Coalville during the dark days of war.

It seems hard to imagine Coalville without its coal mines, but it is encouraging to observe the success of the new Snibston Discovery Park on the site of Snibston Colliery. There is a great potential here to display something of the rich local coal-mining history as Coalville moves into a new era without coal.

We are indebted to Maurice Woodward for setting down on paper just a little of this history for posterity.

It is a pleasure to acknowledge the many who have helped create this publication. Leicestershire Area N.U.M. funded the initial transfer of the manuscript on to a word processor. The majority of the photographs published here have been kindly reproduced from the archives of British Coal. Additional pictures have been provided by Mrs Jan King (on pp. 24 & 25), Jim Clarke (p. 63) and Brian Buck (p. 95). Steph Mastoris of Leicestershire Museums, Arts & Records Service has kindly undertaken the final editing and seen this book through the press. Lastly, but by no means least, thanks go to all our friends and acquaintances for helpful advice, and to all those who have given encouragement during the writing of this book.

John Crocker
Loughborough
August 1993

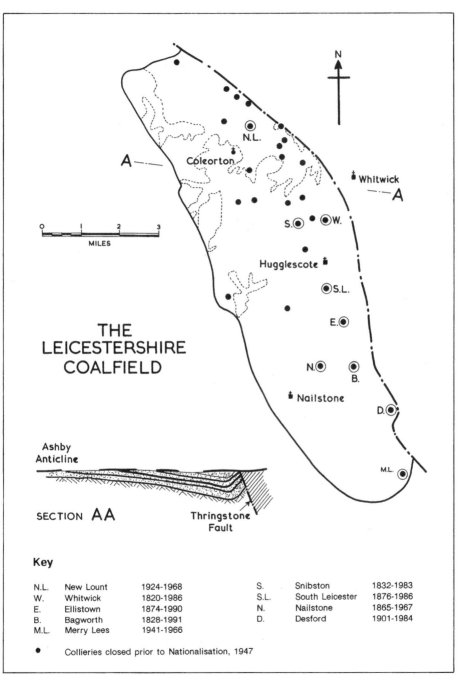

N

THE LEICESTERSHIRE COALFIELD

0   1   2   3
MILES

N.L.

Coleorton

Whitwick

A

A

S. W.

Hugglescote

S.L.

E.

N. B.

Nailstone

D.

M.L.

Ashby
Anticline

SECTION AA

Thringstone
Fault

Key

N.L.	New Lount	1924-1968	S.	Snibston	1832-1983
W.	Whitwick	1820-1986	S.L.	South Leicester	1876-1986
E.	Ellistown	1874-1990	N.	Nailstone	1865-1967
B.	Bagworth	1828-1991	D.	Desford	1901-1984
M.L.	Merry Lees	1941-1966			

●   Collieries closed prior to Nationalisation, 1947

The Leicestershire coalfield (copyright John Crocker).

Coalville in 1927 (Crown copyright reserved).

Chapter One

My Childhood & Early Years at Snibston Colliery

CHILDHOOD

My story is a personal one and deals with the unprecedented changes which have taken place in the mining industry during the last 60 years, not only on the industrial scene, but also in the social patterns of life, and to miners themselves who have had to cope with many struggles from within the industry.

Being a miner, of mining stock, my recollections of the great changes which have affected the coal mining industry around Coalville go back to the 1920s. How different things were then, compared with today's affluence! Indeed, who would have thought in those pre-war years that before the end of this century all deep coal mining would have finished in the Leicestershire Coalfield. Coalville was built on coal, but now this thriving industry is only a memory. Many people will be glad to see the end of all the dirt and smell and subsidence, but to those, like myself, who spent their working life in coal mining, it was an integral part of our existence. So it is only natural that my story should begin with my earliest recollections.

Born the son of a miner, with brothers and uncles also miners, it was taken for granted that I was destined for the pits just like other boys of the district in similar circumstances. Little did we know of the long arduous life that was to follow, and somehow, being young we were oblivious to the tell-tale tragedy all around us. Although poverty and depression abounded in our community, we only became aware of it as we grew older.

My life began in Margaret Street, Coalville, in the year 1923. In those days being born the sixth child in a family of nine was itself a handicap. Mothers handed things down from one child to the next, so clothes and shoes were often worn out when they were passed on. There was nothing else for it, the money just was not there for new things; if the pits only worked two days, miners were only paid two days and very little money at that. My first pair of new shoes however came from an unexpected source – out of the promotions of the two Leicester evening newspapers which were each pressing to extend their circulation. The *Leicester Evening Mail* was offering half a tea-service to their regular readers, whilst "Auntie Suzie" from the *Leicester Mercury* would come into the schools with new shoes from time to time. Many a Monday morning my mother accompanied us to school to take advantage of this offer. On the way she would pop into Dickie Whitford's, the pawnbroker, to borrow money on my father's suit for essentials and to feed us for the coming week. A pawnbroker's ticket was given which was to be redeemed at the weekend by repayment of the borrowed amount plus the money-lender's charge. Many were the times I was hustled out to the pawn shop to redeem one of my father's possessions which he needed on Saturday or Sunday. This was the poverty trap parents found themselves ensnared in and had to endure – an environment we grew up in with little knowledge of any other.

Growing up in Coalville as a boy in the 1920s was very different from today. If one had a penny on Saturday morning, it was spent going to the pictures in the afternoon. This was the age of the silent movies. *Maria Martin, Sweeny Todd the*

Harry Underwood, a Snibston coal merchant leaving the pit yard with a load of 'Snibston Best' house coal, about 1928. He is seen leading carthorse "Daisy" over the landsale weighbridge with weighman Jack Fletcher looking out of the window. In the background is the lamp cabin with the barometer on the outside wall in a long wooden box. Harry was typical of the coal merchants of his day, some running a one-man business, others with either a son or a brother. He only sold 'Snibston best' coal and worked until his death in 1939, when he was struck by a motor cycle and side-car whilst taking his horse and cart back to the field off Belvoir Road. In this picture, Harry would be about 59 years old.

demon barber and Charlie Chaplin were the hits of the day. Sound was provided by an accompanying pianist who displayed some originality in his music; though often, when he was not in step with the film, it was very laughable. These silent films were later followed by Al Jolson in the first talking pictures. In those days, the Grand was the picture house for these movies, followed by the Olympia which had previously been a music hall. The Olympia was later pulled down to be replaced by the Regal; then came the Rex cinema, also in Marlborough Square. The Grand stood on the east side of Belvoir Road opposite Marlborough Square having originally been the corn exchange of the old market. Christmas time at the Grand was special. Santa Claus would give every child an apple or orange, and for an extra penny you could dip in Santa's lucky bag for a present; often this was the only present we had. Both new cinemas extended on to land which was once Coalville's cattle market. As very small boys we would sit on the pens to watch the cows, sheep and pigs being auctioned. It was a really big market extending from the side of Margaret Street Working Men's Club to Owen Street, but the market ceased to exist on this site round about 1930 when the new cattle market was built in Memorial Square.

In the early 1930s, as nine and ten year old boys, we would dash out of school every Thursday to meet the cattle train at Mantle Lane goods depot, where maybe 16 or so young steers would disembark accompanied by two drovers. This was how the weekly joint came into town – on the hoof so to speak. Refrigeration was practically unknown to the smaller butchers and the livestock was slaughtered as required. Many a butcher's shop had a field adjoining the premises where the animals were kept. The Co-op were into every kind of retail business in Coalville before the war and had their own abattoir down Ashby Road. The drovers had to drive the livestock to this slaughter-house and always looked for us boys to help out. Some days the young steers would create havoc as they seemed to sense this was their last journey. One or two would dash down entries between the terraced houses in near panic, so we would have to follow to root them out; it was no joke meeting one which had turned round and was charging back. To us, however, it was an adventure, and there were always a few sweets as our reward.

Even the circus in those days came to town the same way, unloading everything at the railway depot. Every animal except the caged ones had to walk or be carried through Coalville to the circus ground at the top of Margaret Street. This created a real carnival atmosphere with elephants holding the tail of the one in front, snakes carried round the necks of their handlers, big bears chained and muzzled, performing horses plus all that was the circus. This was all part of the razzamatazz of the circus coming to town. It was a great event and caused much excitement among the younger element. If old enough we would help erect the Big Top – anything to get a free pass to the greatest show in town.

Just after the mid 1930s a Circus with a difference was to excite our lives. Sir Alan Cobham's Flying Circus paid a visit to Coalville, on the Fifteen Acre Field, near the Old Oak Tree, Hugglescote. His famous Flying Flea aeroplane would perform aerial stunts over Coalville, with young ladies strapped to the wings, to advertise and attract crowds. It was very exciting as aviation was still in its infancy in those days, and we rarely saw an aeroplane. To fly round Coalville cost adults five shillings, and children two shillings and sixpence, but that was real money and much more than any of us could afford.

Each year throughout my school days, children in the area whose parents were members of the Co-operative Society were given what we termed the Co-op treat or tea party. From the surrounding villages children would make their way into Coalville for what must have been the biggest tea party in the country. With Coalville possessing two railway stations – the Midland and London & North Western – this meant that those who came into town on the L.N.W.R. line would have further to march, the station being situated near the Fox and Goose hotel and the venue just off Ravenstone Road. What did it matter? This was a high day, a day of sheer enjoyment and pure nostalgia, marching with the brass bands with parents lining the streets. Musical entertainment for the ten thousand children was provided by Snibston Colliery Brass Band, Ibstock Town Band, Ibstock United Band, Hugglescote Town Band and Hugglescote United Band; and to feed this multitude required the provision of: 10,000 pieces of cake, 20,000 biscuits, 10,000 bags of sweets, 12,000 fancy cakes, 14 hams, 70 x 4lb. loaves, 6 tins of tongue, 112lb. of butter, 40 gallons of milk, 3 cwt of sugar, 56lb. of tea, and an extra 12 x 4lb. slabs of cake. Without any shadow of doubt the annual Co-op treat was a day in our young lives to remember and savour for the whole year.

Having passed the Eleven-plus examination, I was only able to pursue my schooling at Secondary Modern level since my parents could not afford the fees for a college education. Before going to Broom Leys Modern School, which was the Grammar School overspill, I was to have six weeks school holiday, spent camping in Charnwood Hills with a school friend. The camp site, on what was Captain Clark's estate, is still visible from the Bulls Head public house beer garden. This was our first camping experience and since we were not allowed to camp on our own we joined up with my brother-in-law-to-be and his four mates, who usually spent their summers camping in a large hut on the Forest. They would cycle to work at Lount Colliery on Monday mornings, leaving the dirty washing at their mother's house in Whitwick and pick it up, washed and ironed, on their way back to camp after a day's work down the pit. When the older lads went off to work on the early shift, we had strict instructions and had to do as we were told. After breakfast, before we did anything else, we were required to wash up all the pots, pans and utensils, make the beds, and clean out the hut which was as big as a cricket pavilion – then we were free to do what we liked. That summer the Sherwood Foresters (Nottinghamshire Regiment) were camping on ground which is now King Edward School playing fields at Castle Rock. We spent most of our time at the Regiment's camp, especially in the cook-house when the troops were on manoeuvres. There was always something interesting to do as the men were keen to show us around and teach us Morse-code.

As Coalville's prosperity grew and the town expanded, a Community Hospital of its own became the town's biggest dream and the ambition of everyone from all walks of life. To raise money for the hospital the Coalville Flower Show was born and enjoyed great success in the late 30s, but the Second World War put an end to this fund raising and the ambition of the hospital was never fulfilled. The Flower Show was without doubt one of the biggest at that time and one year even made the Movietone news at the cinema; it was strange to sit in the flicks and see news made in our local backyard on the screen.

This was the biggest occasion in Coalville's calendar, when all people joined together to organise the parades, field events, and other attractions. It was held in the big field known locally as "The John's" off Crescent Road, but formerly during the early 1930s it was held at the rear of the present St.John's ambulance headquarters, Forest Road, Coalville. The great day ended with spectators joining the *Leicester Mercury* push-ball competition. This giant soccer ball would be propelled by hand from one end of the field to the other, over the heads of the crowds. It was one soccer ball that didn't touch the ground.

STARTING WORK

As I lived in Margaret Street, not more than 400 yards from Snibston Colliery, my life was dominated by the sound of the pit buzzer. We were awakened by it, told the time by it, went to school by it, and generally lived under its influence. So it was that when I became 14 in 1937, it was taken for granted that I would descend into the bowels of the earth to begin my working life, just as my father and brothers had done before me. Memories of that first morning at work at "Snibby" are still vividly implanted in my mind: entering the cage (lift) to go underground full of doubts, holding on tightly to the side of the cage, conscious of the great gaping hole beneath me, jokes from the older lads which made me feel the urge to get off even before we had started to move; then a sickening feeling as the cage dropped away, and bang, we had arrived at the pit bottom. The jokes ceased, a few pats on the back from the married men as they left the cage and my initiation was over – I was now one of them.

The first few weeks were spent being taught how to clip (attach) 12 full coal-tubs onto an endless steel rope, walk with them 500 yds. or more to the pit-bottom then return with 12 empty ones. It was really cold in this part of the pit, especially so in the winter months when the icy air rushed into the pit from the downcast shaft. During my first day the time passed so slowly and at snap-time my mate Ronnie Smith, brother of F A Smith (Area union secretary) took me to the warmth of the pit ponies' stables. Ronnie and I remained close friends until his untimely death 24 years later. We had 15 minutes to have our sandwiches and cold tea, but even in that short period we found time to explore the stables, as boys will.

Snibston Colliery surface in the 1930s. A view looking north-west, showing the pit tub circuit, screening sheds (left) and steam shunting locomotive with stationary Snibston coal wagons under the gantry. In the background, in front of the boiler house chimney can be seen the headstocks of the tandem upcast shafts, known as "Smokey" and "Rider", or Nos 2 & 3 shafts. This site was known as Snibston No 2 since the first Stephenson pit was sunk on the other side of the Leicester to Swannington railway. A third pit, Snibston No 3, was also sunk at the top of the Swannington Incline.

"Smokey" shaft was the original ventilating shaft on this site and derived its name from the furnace in the pit bottom, the shaft acting as a chimney drawing air out of the mine workings. Although coal was wound through this shaft, it was not then suitable for men to travel due to the fumes and so they rode the other shaft which at that time was downcast. During the early part of this century both tandem shafts, so named because they were worked in tandem from the same steam winding engine, became upcast when the 'new' main shaft was sunk. The winder house and headstocks associated with this 'new' shaft are seen in the picture right of centre.

Because of the confusion generated by all the Snibston shaft numbers at different pit sites, this shaft was named "Stephenson Shaft", though of course it had nothing to do with the Stephensons!

"French", a Snibston pit pony exhibited at the Derby Royal Show in 1933.

Snibston Colliery had over 50 pit ponies, which were used in the first stage of transportation of the coal from the coal-face to the surface. In the stables we met up with the ostlers – we called them hostlers – who cared for the ponies. They were very dedicated men. Even down the pit these men took pride in their work and every stall was spick and span. Ostler Thomas Toon was one such man. "Soldier", "Boxer", "Ace", "Jack", "Creamy", "Captain", "Ginger", "Rufus", "Billy", "Smut", "Dick", "Rodney", "Turk", "Jasper", "Lion" and "Fly" were just a few names of the ponies, all with a character of their own.

Although the pit only worked two, to two and a half days a week, I was a very proud boy indeed when collecting my wages, and could now go home and put the money on the table, like my elder brothers had done before me. The wages -a few silver coins – were received in a little tin with my tally number on; not much, yet I knew it would help with the family income, for life was really hard. Working and being paid also gave some independence, for instead of having to beg from our parents we now had our own pocket money, and for a sixpence could go on the Sunday train excursions from Coalville to Alton Towers, Trentham Gardens or Rudyard Lake.

The first two years in the pit were years of uncertainty, not knowing if there was work tomorrow for half a day or a full day, or if there was any work at all. As more experience was gained, I was moved away from the pit bottom and early in 1939 was given my first permanent job in a coal-face section (area), one and a half miles "inbye" (away from the pit bottom). This not only brought me into contact with the ponies and their drivers, but also involved me in an innovative system to improve the transportation of coal to the surface. In those days there was no electricity in the coal-face sections, so the system required jigging the full tubs by gravity for three quarters of a mile. There were two ways of doing this. When empty coal tubs came inbye, that is, from the pit bottom to the coal-face ("outbye" is going out of the pit) they were unclipped from the endless steel rope and full tubs of coal clipped on to replace them. Then 12 empties were attached to one end of a tail rope and 12 fulls to the other end; the fulls descended the gradient under gravity, pulling the empties up. Control was provided by means of a braked surge wheel to check the speed of the descending fulls. A safety chain was thrown over the train of fulls, secured from the front tub to the back one; similarly, at the other end of the haulage, 120 yds. away, an empty train had been assembled at the bottom of the gradient. When released, the tubs travelled at terrific speed if allowed to get out of control on the downhill gradient. The other system was to clip full tubs, two at a time, on to an endless steel rope, 20 yds. apart, same with the empty tubs; but here a smaller brake drum and only one operator were required because of the smaller out-of-balance load. Quaint nowadays, but the ingenuity of man seen at its best in the 1930s.

The summer of 1939 brought more short-time working. Being then 16 years old allowed me to draw dole at a shilling a day for the days the pit did not work, but circumstances were to deal us a cruel blow when it came to signing on and paying out. Thursday started the working week for miners pay; it was also the only signing on day at the dole office, but you had to get three waiting days in before claiming benefit. Many a Thursday the pit worked only two hours, with the men knocking off at 9.00 am, which disallowed us any dole that day. No one knew it would be a short day but the dole office knew which pits were working and those not, and they had records of where you worked. If we had not worked the Monday, Tuesday and Wednesday we would have been better off not working those two hours since we lost all dole money for the previous days that week. 'Cruel?', 'Coincidental?' – it happened too many times to be the latter!

WORKING WITH THE PONIES

When war was declared on 3rd September 1939, all this was to change. The older lads in the Territorial Army were called to arms immediately, to be followed by conscription for those 21 years old. These were young men in the prime of life, many of whom worked the pit ponies; and as they departed for the battlefields of Europe they left behind a big gap in the labour force. Along with other boys we became Pony-lads or Pony-drivers. This was a challenge thrust upon us by world events, and the difficult situation the pit suddenly found itself in. "Rodney" was the first pony assigned to me and when entering his stall that morning my apprehensions were considerable as I wondered what sort of temperament he had and whether he would accept so young a master. But my fears were soon dispelled as he nudged his head into my chest. We soon became great pals as he was a very friendly pony, but all he got that morning was a few pats on the neck as I put on his collar and hood, and put the bit between his teeth. Then one last drink of water at the trough and we were on our way. That first morning we soon realised why "Soldier" had the reputation of being a disagreeable cuss. He was the outstanding character of them all with his wily old ways, and as we approached 'wooden junction' he got down to his daily ritual of scratching by rubbing himself on the supports. No one dared get near him till he had finished. It was really funny, also very dangerous in that confined space, while other ponies and drivers queued behind him. It only needed the rope to start up at 7.00 am to incite them all to surge forward, and woe betide anyone who got in the way!

I soon became attached to "Rodney", and many a tit-bit like carrots or fallen apples would find their way into my snap bag. The labour shortage meant that there were not enough drivers to man all the ponies so we found ourselves having to work two stalls instead of one. It was in this transition from boys to men that we had to grow up mighty fast to cope with the new and dangerous responsibilities; during the first few weeks there were three ponies killed by roof cave-in, runaways or by lack of experience.

A few weeks went by and my first tangle with my supervisor, the deputy, erupted. "Rodney" had been out working on the night-shift rota and was not to leave the stables on the day shift till 7.30 am. I pleaded with the ostlers to take

"French", a South Leicester pit pony exhibited at the Derby Royal Show in 1933.

"Sailor", a South Leicester pit pony exhibited at the Ashby Show in 1933.

him off the night-shift, explaining that being out all night and then having to work two stalls on the day shift was cruelty to the poor animal, but they could not, or would not do this. The system was patently wrong and needed changing. The deputy cursed me for the lost time involved since I had to wait over until 7.30 am then work a tired pony; if the pony died it would be the pony-lad's fault. I could not win and again spoke out my indignation, emphasising the cruelty being inflicted on him through over-work. After the third time of my complaining, they began to see reason, standing "Rodney" over in an old roadway till 10.45 am, then working him till 2.30 pm. And from my point of view, was it necessary for me to work two ponies at a time instead of one? There was a saying: half a loaf is better than none, so the situation was accepted.

As the weeks and months passed by we became seasoned hands with the ponies, but after Dunkirk, when more young men went off to war, these were replaced in the pits by 14, and 15-year-old boys. They were put to work with very little experience on other jobs, and such was the desperate labour situation that they too became pony-lads at this youthful age. It became a real pit rodeo with between 19 and 21 ponies deployed in 51's section. Apart from "Soldier" and "Rodney" some of the other ponies were: "Boxer", "Ace", "Jack", "Captain", "Creamy", "Ginger", "Rufus", "Billy", "Lion", "Fly", "Dick", "Smut", "Turk", and my own special favourite "Jasper". The inexperience among the new pony-lads brought further casualties to the ponies as it took a long time for them to learn one another's habits and idiosyncrasies. The pony "Jack" had his eye torn out in an unfortunate accident, but it was when he was returned underground that we had most cause for alarm. Following a few months on the surface convalescing in the sunshine, "Jack" came back to become a demon pony with his kicking and squealing, his mind seemingly possessed by the devil.

After "Rodney" I drove "Lion" and "Dick", then was told one day to fetch "Jasper". His driver had been a 15-year-old; they had not got on very well and the scars on his back-side showed the lack of experience of his driver. To get the best out of one's pony you had to see he was properly tackled and looked after. "Jasper" was very temperamental and frightened from past experiences. He would rush forward at certain points in our journeys to and from the coal-face. To gain his confidence I shared with him almost everything I took to eat; gradually it worked and he became much more settled. This was as well for later on my patience was to be rewarded. One day coming down a steep gradient we had a runaway pony with two full coal-tubs behind us. A locker (a brake stick placed in the spokes of the tub wheel) in the back tub had broken and many a pony had panicked in similar circumstances and was killed. In my haste to get clear I tripped and was left in complete darkness. My cries "Whoa Jasp! Whoa Boy!" were of desperation rather than hope; but my pony held although we both finished up in a tangled heap. In that confined space I reached for his head to try and console him, for between the two of us it was difficult to say who was the most frightened. After what seemed like an eternity, help came to our assistance. That was the first of many lives given back to me working in the coal-mines, this one owed to my pony "Jasper".

Fifty one's section stall system at that time comprised the pilot stall and galleries, or level roadways, on either side of this stall. The object was to open up new stalls as workings advanced, thus creating new galleries 50 yds. apart, first on the right, then on the left of its own roadway. To describe it more accurately would be to liken the whole section to a semi-circle of coal, with 51's stall punching its way forward in the centre, the other stalls advancing at specified distances behind. From the extreme stall on the right, maybe two or three galleries below, you could gain access to the next stall, until you reached the last one on the opposite side. This was also the pattern of the ventilation system and the escape route in case of emergencies. Situated in the galleries would be wooden ventilation doors, which deflected air round the section. As we had to pass to and fro through these doors there had to be a method of preventing air by-passing the coal-face when these doors were opened, so a second door would be installed 20 yds. from the first one to ensure one door remained closed at all times. Any misuse would short-circuit the ventilation and could have serious consequences.

We pony-lads would ride the limbers (steel shafts into which the ponies were harnessed) along the galleries with both full tubs and empty ones. Depending on the direction we travelled the ponies would nudge open the doors to save us the job. A draw bar welded underneath each coal-tub enabled a steel connecting bar to fit between the limbers and the tub, secured by a limber peg. Many a pony-

Materials handling with ponies at South Leicester Colliery, 1959. An example of the use of pit-ponies in getting supplies inbye where there was no haulage system. The pony is seen dragging an arch section with one man holding the back end to balance the load. The front end of the arch is lashed to the pony's limbers, and properly executed this was not a dangerous operation even in restricted spaces as seen here. On the right is the drive end of the conveyor, with its associated electrical control panels on the left and power cables tied up overhead.

lad, having lost his limber peg, would use a large nail; but this was a dangerous practice and not officially permitted. Riding the limbers to and from the stalls was also dangerous and likewise not the accepted way of travelling the roads; but we had it off to a fine art, crouching on the limber cross bar. To do it effectively, we would fit half a cocoa tin over our shukie lamps so that the light would be projected forward in front of the pony's head. He could then only see what was in front of him and would not know where his driver was. It was a battle of wits, and such was the relationship between pony and driver that formed the basis of successful combinations.

The ponies themselves were characters in their own right. "Ginger" and "Creamy", so named from the appearance of their coats, were two powerful and outstanding individuals. "Captain" acquired his name by his majestic manner. "Rodney", "Dick", "Rufus", "Ace" and "Turk" were stocky, hard-as-iron ponies, as if specially bred for the pits, and "Boxer" was a powerful but dangerous pony. My old pal "Jasper", with his beautiful silky coat, was highly temperamental but very intelligent. Then there was poor old "Smut" -age and wear-and-tear in the pit had taken its toll and his arthritic legs would give way if he stood still for any period of time. But whatever their individual characters, each one had a special instinctive awareness of the particular dangers underground. They could, and did, warn their drivers of imminent danger, especially in the case of roof movements and falls, for they were by far the more experienced of the working partnerships. Even some of their habits were near human. Many a lad would have his snap (sandwiches) stolen out of his jacket pocket by the crafty ponies. When caught in the act the ponies were still allowed an extra tit-bit. It was really funny at times, but not so if the pony had eaten your food; however we would all share our snap with the victim, and this was the bond which existed in the pits. "Jasper" and I continued awhile longer but then I was to leave the pit to further my working life at New Lount Colliery.

During my journeys to the coal-face I came to the heart and soul of the pit; here men were lying on their sides in the stalls (coal-face workings) labouring by candlelight, hand-holing (undercutting the coal) with a pick, taking two inches of dirt under the coal-seam prior to blasting and filling. This was the process of extracting coal at that time. "Snibby" was a family pit, where father and sons worked side by side, but my greatest surprise was to find these were the very same men who had imposed their own culture on our local community. The Benistons and Rowells, among others, belonged to Snibston Colliery brass band and played in Coalville park most Sunday evenings. Like other townsfolk I often visited the park to listen to them playing and enjoyed their various renderings of popular music. If those people in the park could have seen the working conditions the players had to endure they would not have believed they were the same men.

C.Bradford, A.Colver and W.Kendrick, led by Colliery Manager Jabez Emmerson, belonged to the cricket team and, most Sunday afternoons and

At work on the Yard Seam, Snibston Colliery, 1936. Bill Wilkinson (left) setting a timber support ("spragging") as he advanced by hand-holing the dirt under the coal; Stan Kendrick (centre) trimming the loose coal on the face with a pick to prevent accidental falls, and George Marsden (right) setting a wooden roof support (pit-prop) with a six-pound hammer. The naked "shukie" (carbide) lamp hooked to the wooden support is the only illumination at the coal-face.

Stan, now 83 years old, relates that as a 27-year-old married man, living in Ibstock five miles away from Snibston Colliery, he would cycle to work, leaving home at 5.15 a.m. to be down the pit by 6.00 a.m. From the pit-bottom he then had to walk underground three quarters of the way back towards Ibstock to his workplace. Even his wife found this hard to believe, but it was no exaggeration.

Prayers at the coal-face, Snibston Colliery, at 11 o'clock on 11th November 1936. George Marsden (Chargeman), Stan Kendrick, Arthur Grew and Bill Wilkinson with heads bowed in silent prayer remembering the dead of the First World War. This was the custom in all walks of life until the Second World War.

A full coal tub has been brought into the gate-road for transportation out of the pit, and to prevent it running away a "josh", or wedge, has been placed under the axle. Davy lamps in the hands of two of the men were mainly used for testing for the presence of methane gas. On the right of the photograph a stone pack can be seen. This has been built after coal extraction to support the roof and strengthen the roadway. Note also the men's attire: no knee pads to cushion the impact when working on their knees, no safety boots or protective clothing, and no cap lamps! These men were in the process of developing Snibston Colliery's first long-wall coal-face ("Monty") in the Yard Seam.

evenings during the summer, delighted all with their commitment to our national game. T.Deacon, "Cag" and T.Brownlow, "Big Bertie" Kendrick, "Neaker" Squires, "Cubby" Fern and a host of others played in the public house soccer teams. They formed the basis of the successful teams, though not all the players were miners. Yes, many public houses had soccer teams and, as an 11-year-old boy, it was my job to mark the pitch with sawdust for 'Snibston New Inn' team, which my father ran. The 'Engineers Arms' and 'Old Vics' were two other teams which spring to mind. Most surprising of all was finding men who preached the Gospel in our local and village chapels. How could men work in such appalling conditions and still preach Christianity? Or was it these conditions that strengthened their faith? Knowing the Baptist, Ebenezer, Wesleyan and Methodist chapels only by name, it never occurred to me the occupation of those who preached the sermons. The Saddingtons were a typical mining family in this respect. As it was in the pit, so this side of life too was part and parcel of growing up; while some men played others prayed. Death came to the unlucky ones. My first recollection is still with me when two brothers carried their injured brother out one day. I was standing at my pony's head while they passed, and as they paused to change over a hand reached for mine and a voice from the stretcher spoke my name. I took the hand and looked towards his brothers. Their grim faces told the seriousness of the situation: he was to die before reaching the surface. When arriving home that day I wanted no dinner, my mother understood for bad news travelled fast. The very next morning made me realize what part women played in our lives, for after such a tragedy father and sons were back at work, hewing coal in the same stall their kinsman was struck down the day before. A few days after I was to ask the ultimate question "Why?". The answer was short and sharp. To have stayed off work would have meant less bread and meat on the table for the living. So men worked and women mourned.

The men in the coal-face stalls – the Benistons, Rowells, Saddingtons, Balls, Foukes and Westons – were a diverse mixture of characters, influenced by their surface activities. My first encounter with a Pentecostal Christian (Ernie Weston) was below ground. Being assigned to his stall one day, I was amazed at the Biblical phrases and sayings written in chalk on the wooden beams which spanned the galleries. I think not one beam escaped his attention.

In contrast to most of the men, Bernard Lord was the pony-lads friend and saviour. When no-one had a fag to smoke, Bernard would nearly always come to the rescue. But not least among the pony-lads friends was the man who ran the section – Joe Whittaker – whose tremendous job of looking after the ponies and the lads, and ensuring that there was full operational continuity, never got him down. His surface interests lay in football where he was actively involved as a soccer referee. Joe was a really nice guy, and never blew the whistle on any of us.

The stalls all had numbers or symbols, so tubs of coal were marked with the identification of the stall from which it came so that it could be identified and weighed on the surface. From these check weights the weekly earnings were derived. All stall men would tip pony-lads as an extra incentive to work hard for them; many a two-bob (2s), half-crown (2/6d) or five-bob (5s) was earned in this fashion. To collect our tips on Fridays, we would make our way to a part of the pit-yard where "butties" (charge hands) divided the money between the men in their stall. The money would be emptied out of a tin, put into four equal parts, four men to a stall, then a piece of coal or stone placed on each part to prevent the pound and 10s notes blowing away in rough winds. This way each man could see that he was not being cheated by the Buttie. In those days, such was the quaint way for men to collect their wages.

In 1942 I moved to New Lount Colliery. It was very hard leaving mates, ponies and familiar surroundings, for we had developed a real bond, bound together by tragedies and war. After moving, I still remained in the Home Guard platoon during the rest of the war, for "Snibby" had a great platoon of part-time soldiers. In 1944 a number of these lads from the platoon were involved in the Snibston cage tragedy. It was rumoured that both cages had crashed to the pit-

Snibston Colliery surface, 1957. Looking north from the pit bank which grew bigger and bigger as the years went by. This picture shows the old screening sheds (left) with tippler house centre foreground. Empty tubs on the gantry are returning to the shaft. The ventilation air casings can be seen over the Smokey and Rider shafts, whilst the Stephenson downcast shaft is uncluttered by air-locks making coal winding much easier.

Joe Whittaker with "Jim" at Snibston Colliery, 1954. Joe Whittaker was Foreman (Doggie) with responsibility for the ponies and pony-lads underground. The ponies were brought to the surface for the annual holiday shutdown and put out to grass on the Snibston Grange fields. "Jim" is wearing a leather hood for his protection in confined spaces underground, and to concentrate his vision forward. Doggies like Joe were paid an extra 3d a day for their supervisory responsibilities.

bottom, but it turned out to be an overwind (cages not stopping in their normal position). Even so, one cage did smash into the bottom landing, loaded with two decks of men and boys. Although no deaths occurred many of the cage occupants finished up in Leicester Royal Infirmary with broken legs and other serious injuries, and one young man never worked again.

To give an insight into the humour of coal-miners in difficult and painful situations I quote a joke concerning this incident, told by Bill Moorhouse ("Meffer") to a colleague in the next hospital bed, Frank Fantom ("Spud").

Vicar: "How far did you fall my good man?"

Patient: "Above half-way vicar."

Vicar: "The Lord must have been with you my good man."

Patient: "No bloody fear vicar, we were going wrong road for him."

Chapter Two
With the Home Guard

SOME ADVENTURES IN "DAD'S ARMY"

At the declaration of war with Germany on 3rd September 1939, the young men in the Territorials were called to arms immediately, to be followed by conscription for the 21 year olds. The Territorials were a part-time civilian army, many of whom were miners from the local pits, especially "Snibby", and had received basic training with the Regular Army. In those days when there was no such thing as an annual week's holiday, it was a great adventure and a pleasant change to go up to Catterick in Yorkshire on these training exercises. But such was the need at the outbreak of war that these trained civilians were drafted immediately, regardless of occupation. These demands for able bodied men meant that, along with other boys of my age, we had to fill the gap left by their departure; but it was in the following year after Dunkirk (26th May to 4th June 1940) that my adventures in the Home Guard began. When some of these same young men returned home, having been defeated by the mighty German armies in France, I was called upon to help defend my country and so joined the Local Defence Volunteers at the pit.

The prime object of the L.D.V. was to guard places of work such as pits and factories. The first recruits, among them many elderly men, stood guard with anything they could lay their hands on for weapons – sticks, pitchforks, shotguns – and gave rise to a great deal of good humoured ribaldry. We were known as the "Look, Duck and Vanish brigade", or else the "Long Dentured Volunteers". We had no uniforms or equipment in those early days and marched and counter-marched in our own civilian clothes; slope arms, order arms and present arms were all executed with the aid of a 4ft. wooden pole similar to a sweeping brush handle. And so emerged the legendary "Dad's Army". It was a few months afterwards that we were eventually fitted out with uniforms and American 'Remington or Springfield P.17 rifles, along with a few bayonets and one Thompson sub-machine gun (the "tommy-gun"), but no ammunition. With this change in our fortunes we became known officially as the Home Guard. Thus I became a private in the Colliery Platoon, attached to 'C' Company 5th Battalion, Leicestershire Regiment – nicknamed the "Tigers" after their badge which commemorated regimental service in India.

Battalion structure consisted of a thousand or more men, sub-divided into five Companies commanded by a Major or Captain, and further sub-divided into Platoons with a First Lieutenant as Commanding Officer and a Second Lieutenant as Platoon Officer. In 1941, as the scare of invasion receded, the

Snibston Colliery Home Guard Platoon, 1940-1945. On the back row are (l-r); Pte A.Haywood, Pte A.Bevan, Pte A.Toon, Pte K.Staines, Pte G.Smith, Lcp W.Avery, Pte E.Davis, Pte J.Clarke, Pte G.Lager, Pte B.Kendrick and Pte D.Staines. On the next row are; Pte M.Woodward, Pte F.Keeling, Pte M.Straw, Pte A.Peace, Pte K.Pollard, Pte H.Moore, Pte B.Edwards, Pte G.Haywood, Pte B.Baker and Pte R.Bates. On the next row are; Pte J.Combes, Lcp C.Bradford, Pte E.Davis, Lcp N.Lee, Cp J.Burton, Cp J.Springthorpe, Lcp A.Edwards, Cp G.Price, and Pte C.Bywater On the front row are; Cp D.Millership, Sgt L.Nichols, 2nd Leut Lovett, 2nd Leut G.Shilliam, Major Clamp, 1st Leut W.Hill, Sgt G.Manders, Sgt S.Meakin, Sgt W.Wildgoose and Sgt Mjr Remington.

elderly were asked to stand down and we became an infantry battalion. Training was to the army manual and Captain Wilson, a regular army officer, was mainly responsible for this. For a start we stood guard at the pit gates on a rota system when the work place was most vulnerable -from 12 noon on Saturday until 10pm on Sunday. There was no official guard during the week as the risk of sabotage was minimised by the presence of many workmen and officials involved in their round-the-clock routine pit activities. In those early days practically every pit and factory had a contingent of the Home Guard and those who found themselves without an establishment joined the nearest unit.

EARLY DAYS

With the disastrous battles that had taken place in Europe, the British Army Manual had to be re-written. The German invasion of France, with their armies outflanking France's 'impregnable' Maginot Line of defence, followed by the heroic British rearguard action at Dunkirk, had been humiliating defeats. So it was along the lines of this new thinking that we were to be trained. To comply with this, our platoon was divided into three squads, with Platoon Headquarters at Snibston Colliery. Each squad, when on parade, answered to No.1 rifleman, No.2 rifleman and so on; two squads had a Lewis machine gun with No.1 gunner and No.2 gunner (we actually had only two gunners early on). We were taught battle attack formation – how to take objectives by advancing one squad at a time while covering fire was provided by the other two. It was some time before we got live ammunition for the rifles, so we had to practise loading, aiming, and firing with dummy rounds. It became a real bore, until one day the Commanding Officer informed us that he had managed to get hold of some genuine ammunition. He had us 'bused out to a small firing range at Ashby, about five miles away. There were only three small targets there, but at least we could fire live ammunition for a change. I must confess my first shot didn't even find the target. The recoil from firing live rounds was very different from firing dummy ones, and certainly different from firing at the local fair-ground, which was a permanent feature at the bottom of Owen Street. Nevertheless I was credited with three scores in the inner target and like to think these were all mine, and that no-one was hitting my target instead of his own! Anyway, it was an experience which stood us in good stead for later on when we had more opportunities to practise with real bullets.

We were called on parade Wednesday night and Sunday morning, so it was mostly Sunday for these activities. Military vehicles were not involved in local movements; the Midland Red and other private 'bus companies were glad of the work since their revenue was reduced by curtailed services which ceased altogether after 9.00 pm. Shifts at the pit were from 7.00 am to 2.30 pm, 2.30 pm to 10.00 pm and 10.30 pm to 6.00 am. The Home Guard parades took place between 10.00 am and 12.30 pm on Wednesday and Sunday mornings, but on Sundays anything – special parades, platoon or company exercises, or even involvement with battalion manoeuvres – could happen at any time, continuing until the exercise was completed or you were dismissed.

It was about this time, in the spring of 1941, when we were again 'bused out one morning to an old disused clay-hole near Measham, where we were instructed in firing the Northolt Projector. This was an ancient weapon originating from the 1914-18 war or just afterwards, mounted on a tripod and used for firing hand grenades. As you withdrew the safety pin from the grenade you had to keep it intact by keeping pressure on the lever. Then you inserted the grenade into the barrel. The side of the barrel kept the lever in position until the grenade was fired. As the grenade left the barrel, the lever detached and activated the detonator. The distance projected was not great and most of us were unimpressed with this piece of gadgetry, for in our opinion we could throw them further, particularly the live grenades that gave you an added incentive to get them as far away as possible.

Snibston Colliery pit yard, 1963. This was the wartime parade ground of the Snibston Colliery Platoon of the Home Guard. It was also the place where, before the war, we received our wages in a little tin which was handed back through the pay window (second from the rear) when we had emptied it. The Butties received a lump payment for all of the men in their stall, in one tin, and then shared it out amongst them on the ground. The picture shows the rescue room, landsale office and first-aid room, also the hose drying rig of the old Coalville Fire Station on the opposite side of Ashby Road (extreme right).

One of our first contacts with the British Army was with a local searchlight battery at the top of Altons Hill. Having been bombed out of their home station at the Rolls Royce factory in Derby they were moved into the countryside on high ground between Coalville and Ashby. Their tactics were changed, with improved co-ordination between the different batteries giving better coverage of the sky over strategic targets. On our first visit we were given a tour round the site to be shown the searchlights and machine-gun emplacements. There were no "ack-ack" guns on this site – it was only a searchlight unit – with the machine-guns for self defence. The sergeant in charge explained how, with the new tracking equipment, they could actually 'see' sound reflected from an enemy plane and were able to follow its course so the lights could find and follow the target. This was 50 years ago – a fascinating new discovery at that time! In the late autumn and winter months of 1940, we received instructions in the machine gun emplacements, but not on the light itself; although having received this training we never took part in any real activities of the unit. However, we became very friendly with the personnel and this friendship developed, so that later on we were always given an invitation to the E.N.S.A. concert party whenever they were visiting their site. Having been given hot drinks and supper on these occasions, the same question was always asked of us: "You're coming again next time?" It was the only time the regular lads got supper, so how could we possibly refuse! This became a standing joke between us. I am sure all of us in the platoon enjoyed these nights for there was little else to do. But as we marched home on these late nights in the rain, sometimes in the snow, the stark realities of the times we were living in began to sink home for, approaching the pit-gates, we knew full well we had to be down there again by 7 o'clock next morning.

WEEKEND CAMPS AND MANOEUVRES

When the next year came round we were to go on a long weekend camp. The Whitsuntide holiday away from the pit seemed a good idea at the time, so we were marched out on the Saturday to a camp near the searchlight unit. We were allocated bags of straw (so-called palliasses) to sleep on; then so many were assigned to each nissen hut – concrete floors in every one. Training was cut down to about three hours on Saturday, but on Sunday it was up bright and early and out on manoeuvres for most of the day. At other times these manoeuvres usually took place in open countryside around Coalville, but trenching by our own platoon took place on the pit-bank, which because of its elevation provided a good vantage point. We were allowed out at night, but had to be back in camp at a certain time. For entertainment in those days, we always 'captured' the nearest pub with a piano – the Angel at Coleorton, Robin Hood and Station Inn at Swannington, and the Waggon and Horses at Coalville were always popular – where a good old fashioned sing-song was sure to follow. Wherever we went the locals were very friendly; still, were we not all in this together? After a good night and in spite of everything, everyone went home happy. So back to camp and our palliasses, a few more hours training on the Monday morning, then the march back home. Some holiday! But there was nothing else to do and it was a change.

With the war going badly in the early days, our training was stepped up as the threat of invasion loomed. We were 'bused out one Sunday morning to go on an Army assault course. When we approached the destination near Appleby Magna, our platoon Second Lieutenant ordered everyone out to attack this base as a 'hostile' objective. While others drove on and through the front gates, we were formed up to attack from the rear. We went across the fields, along the ditches, up the hedgerows until eventually we arrived at where the Regular Army men were putting the finishing touches to the assault course we were to use later, and surrounded them. After their initial surprise at being 'captured' they really saw the funny side of things, a few jokes, a bit of leg pulling, but no one complained. Wasn't this what training was all about? It was on this occasion that our Second Lieutenant was seen in a new light, for given the first opportunity he put the book-theories into practice. Through this approach he earned our added respect. After a rest we went on to take the assault course last; the one and only time we led from the rear.

Another, not so humorous occasion was being called out on night manoeuvres. Our orders were to report for duty on Saturday night at 10.00 pm. We assembled in the pit-yard and were marched out to an unknown destination, which turned out to be Holly Hayes wood at Whitwick, in those days mostly surrounded by fields. Here the N.C.O.s informed us that the exercise was to take up positions in the wood and stop any infiltration by the 'enemy', so we were posted at strategic points around the perimeter. As I stood with my back to a stone wall in total darkness, the sounds of foxes, owls and other woodland creatures made it very spooky indeed; to make matters worse as the night wore on the heavens opened and down came the rain. What had been a beautiful summer evening was turning into a terror of a night. Time seemed endless, as wristwatches for us were a thing for the future. At the first break of dawn the whole exercise was called off and we were marched back home amid murmurings and grumbles. Since my retirement I have walked through the same wood on numerous occasions. There is still the same peace and tranquillity, but as the sun goes down and dusk begins to fall I hasten away, with a little shudder and a smile to myself as the old memories flood back.

Our second weekend camp soon came round the following year. This time we were 'bused out to Gopsall Hall, a stately home in the countryside, occupied by a unit of the Royal Army Ordinance Corp. We were to be under canvas, but the area where the tents had been pitched was waterlogged. Eventually we were billeted in one of the many magnificent rooms of the Hall which were completely bare. I guess there were as many as 40 of us to a room; sleep was absolutely impossible. What a life! The next morning was bathed in brilliant sunshine when we made our way to the mess tent. Breakfast consisted of bacon, baked beans, sausage meat, fried bread, white bread and a mug of tea. It was a breakfast such as we had not had since the war began and everyone enjoyed it immensely. When the orderly officer came round with his – "Any complaints?" – I'm sure all of us could have spoken out for more, as it seemed we were always hungry. No one did so, such was army discipline. We were allowed half an hour to assemble before being given our orders.

The 'enemy' had occupied a spinney just over half a mile away; we were to flush them out and secure the ground beyond. Our own 'C' company was to spearhead this operation with supporting units in the rear and on the flanks. As other units moved into their positions we concentrated on camouflage to try and blend in with the countryside. Our Second Lieutenant was 'on the ball' as usual, this time with good reason for we had an audience! Midland Area Command, which included "top brass" from the Army, were to observe the whole operation. When the whistle went to commence we got off to a good start, but our inexperience began to tell as we neared our objective. We advanced, the last part flat on our stomachs with someone somewhere up front creating a lot of noise and smoke; it was like all hell let loose and was most realistic. The combination of exercise and smoke left one decidedly queasy; it was as well that we had not asked for second helpings at breakfast! However, when it was all over, the feedback was that the "top brass" had been highly impressed and had retired in good spirits. Monday soon came round when we were again 'bused home, back to work down the pit on Tuesday morning, another long weekend gone. This was our life, what was there really to grumble about – we had all been well fed!

As the next weekend camp came round we all had mixed feelings, but come what may we would eat well. This time we had wooden huts to sleep in – a bit of a change from the bare boards of the stately home and the concrete floor of the nissen huts. Next morning (Sunday) was again the day for an important exercise with a unit of the Regular Army. This time we were to defend, so were placed at strategic points for this operation. It was also more amusing to us this time as we were static with the attackers doing all the hard slogging. The sun beat down mercilessly that morning and we began to feel sympathy for the opposition. Their final attack succeeded in taking our position, but they were absolutely whacked when the final whistle blew. About 15 minutes were allowed before they regrouped and in this time together we enjoyed a smoke with the same old jokes and stories. No hostility or resentment was displayed, for them the real thing was to come later. From time to time the Platoon was also engaged in mock battle exercises in residential areas to simulate street fighting and orders were given not to trample anyone's cabbage patch. On these occasions "top brass" observers were usually in attendance to prevent things getting out of hand rather than to check our efficiency.

Our time was not entirely spent in training, on manoeuvres or on guard, for from time to time throughout the war the King called the country to a National day of Prayer to pray for all the armed services on land, sea and in the air, for their deliverance, and to unite the country in the common cause. So it was on the first church parade on those Sunday mornings that I became aware what other people were doing as part of the war effort. On parade were all the other voluntary units – Air Raid Wardens, St John's Ambulance, Auxiliary Nurses, Auxiliary Fire Service, Special Constabulary, Air Training Corps, Air Cadets, Observer Corps, and all other units attached to Civil Defence. I recognised some of the women and girls who worked in munition factories around town. During the war, local factories, institutions and warehouses were requisitioned to provide manufacturing facilities for the war effort. Munition units sprang up in any tumble-down shed,

Whitwick Colliery No.3 winding engine during electrification, 1955. The new winding engine house is nearing completion and the steam winder is still in use. With the nationalisation of the coal industry in 1947 electrification of steam winding engines became a top priority around the country.

outbuilding, classroom or garage that was not otherwise contributing to the national effort. Whatever part we played, we were all in it together.

WEAPONS TRAINING

As the months went by we were issued with a crude sort of weapon, the Blacker Bombard. This was a 29mm spigot-mortar, basically a barrel with a tube (called the spigot) running up the centre which located the mortar bomb. It was not a very mobile piece of equipment and needed a crew of four to operate. Anti-tank mortar bombs were 26ins long, weighing 20lb.; the anti-personnel bombs weighed 14lb.. I guess it was another useless weapon rejected by the Regular Army, but suitable for the Home Guard to practise with. Having obtained anti-tank mortar bombs for practice, we set up old railway sleepers from the surrounding pit-yard and piled them three to four feet high on the pit-bank as a target. Here on the pit-bank recovery of the dummy bombs was made easier. Thus we had plenty of practice with the anti-tank weapon to test its range, but could not visualise what the genuine thing would do, nor did we have any

Steam shunting locomotive 0–6–0 "Ellen" at Snibston Colliery, 1957. In the centre of the picture is the new fitting shop and on the left, Margaret Street and the footbridge leading to Ashby Road.

experience with real anti-personnel bombs. However, we got saddled with a large amount of Molotov Cocktails which were the standard anti-personnel grenade of the Home Guard. They were no more than glass bottles, half-filled with petrol with a paraffin-soaked rag for ignition. Later these were replaced by self igniting phosphorus and nitro-glycerine grenades, similarly in glass flasks. All of these were highly inflammable and very dangerous to use and so were never used in practice. They were kept for emergency use and had to be stored well away from any building; and in what better place than the pit-bank? So they got placed in a remote dug-out, remaining there for a long time, partly forgotten.

With the Americans now having entered the war through the treachery of the Japanese bombing of Pearl Harbour in December 1941, weapons and ammunition were beginning to filter through more quickly and we were issued with a small-arms sub-machine gun. This was the mass produced sten-gun, the most common automatic weapon issued to the Home Guard. When the firing pin was worn down the whole bolt was replaced. We made our own firing range with the pit-bank as the background, and since the sten-gun only had a range of 25 to 30yds. there was not much danger to anyone, although of course, even in these circumstances, precautions were always taken. By now we could begin to test the capabilities of our own platoon, but friends around me were becoming disenchanted with the apparent ineffectiveness of our efforts, and asked if I would go with them to volunteer for one of the armed services. Under the Essential Works Order this was impossible, since we were in a reserved occupation. This was our life and had to be so until the end of the war. Some did go to the nearest recruiting office in Leicester, to test the system, but when it came to answering the question about occupation they were shown the door in no uncertain terms when they said they were coal miners.

The next task given to our platoon was to build a hand grenade practice-throwing bay which consisted of a priming bay, throwing bay and observation post. These were sited again on the pit-bank, about 250yds. in a direct line from the top of Owen Street. The task of constructing this was given to the shift-workers, a small number of married men who were on afternoon or night shift spending Wednesday mornings on the task, although some did work on Sunday. The basic materials used to fill the sandbags were obtained from the pit-bank with a lot of hard work and energy expended by those involved, but the finished project was well worthwhile. Dummy grenades were used for the drill before live ones were issued. This was again a new experience, for these things could bite back if a mistake was made. Initially we had more than our share of practice, Sunday after Sunday, but as other units wanted to come to use the facility it was inevitable that we had less throwing time to ourselves. As the others came to test their skills our crew spent more time in the priming bay. This was a small

An 0-6-0 shunting locomotive at Snibston Colliery, 1930s. It is hauling a full load away from the screening plant. As small boys we loved to peer through the railings by the foorbridge at the top of Margaret Street (see p. 37) to watch the shunting activities.

Two Hunslet 0-6-0 shunting locomotives at Snibston Colliery, 1967. They are drawing a train of untreated power station smalls. Two locos are used for safety purposes after runaway accidents at the Belvoir Road crossing. On the uphill run, one loco was placed at the front, hauling the train, and the second was placed at the rear to contain any breakaway incident.

sandbagged area within the throwing complex where grenades were made live by two experienced personnel who fitted the detonators. Under orders of officers in the observation post, an individual went to the priming bay, collected his primed grenade, then went forward to the throwing area to complete the drill.

Competitions were often organised between platoons and companies as spectator events and, in the absence of other public entertainment, they proved popular with the general public as a welcome Saturday afternoon diversion from the rigours of wartime life. One of the favourite events was assembling the Lewis machine-gun on the run. It weighed 26lb., broke down into sub-assemblies for portability and was fed by magazines which jammed if they were not fitted properly. The gun mechanism was equally notorious for jamming, there being set routine procedures for dealing with these problems. The object of the exercise was for each team to cover the 150yds. from A to B carrying the parts of the gun, assemble it the quickest way possible and simulate firing the first round. You had to be involved to appreciate how many things could go wrong, but it was pure entertainment and hilarious fun.

MORE MANOEUVRES

During the summer of 1943 our routine training continued. One day we suddenly received orders to be on parade at 5.45 am the following Sunday morning, when we were again 'bused out to an unknown destination. All we were told was that it would be an all-day manoeuvre where we would be fed in the field. Army food was good compared with civilian rations and there were no complaints at this prospect. We arrived at our destination near Kegworth and were posted close to the river, where we were told to use the long grass at the river-side to make us less conspicuous, and to wait. This turned out to be a long wait, as 'buses were going by in what seemed like a never ending convoy. We crouched and lay in the tall grass for nearly two hours, then it became apparent what the exercise was all about, for coming down the river Soar, we sighted the sappers of the Royal Army Engineers with their floating pontoons. They came down to where we were waiting, but before they manoeuvred their pontoon sections into position to form a bridge-head we were at last told the object of the exercise – we were to make a large scale assault on the other side of the river using the bridges. On completion of the erection of the floating bridges the order came for us to move, which, after waiting all that time, was quite a relief. We crossed the river to the accompaniment of the same old jokes, advancing through all the clamour and smoke again until, about twenty minutes after we had got to the other side, an umpire appeared to tell us we were now declared 'dead'. Our officers were given coloured arm-bands and told to assemble at a certain rendezvous at a given time. I looked back towards the river and was met by an astonishing sight. The number of personnel who had crossed, and those waiting on the other side, was staggering. It was only afterwards that we learnt that most Battalions of the Regiment had taken part, including the 1st, 3rd, 5th, and 8th.

Reflecting back on those moments convinces me of the great effort that was being planned for the following year, but at the time we were not to know about the forthcoming invasion of France. Being 'dead', we captured a public house without much difficulty and they opened before time that morning. Maybe this was all part of the exercise; so we relaxed, for we had another long wait before us, but this time a more enjoyable one. I was just a 20-year old lad then and what was to follow that day made it all worthwhile being in "Dad's Army". This day was the happiest and most hilarious time of the whole five years. First one then another of our party got on the piano, to be joined by others who had suffered the same fate. Events really took off as more and more 'dead men' joined us, spilling out on to the lawns. It became one hell of a party. The entertainment was terrific, the friendship and comradeship was all there, they say dead men tell no tales but 'dead' men drank some beer that morning. This was one of the more pleasurable and humorous sides of the Home Guard. When the order came to be 'bused out, most of us only wanted to lay back in the seats and go to sleep, but this was not to be – we were still on manoeuvres! Halfway home our transport was halted, as the 'enemy' had taken the ground ahead. There was no way forward so we were required to secure the occupied territory before being reunited with our transport. This was a situation we had not bargained on, and it proved more difficult than it should have been, but having completed the task it was 'home sweet home' and straight to bed for me. It had been a crazy day but it had had its moments.

But there were sad moments and frightening times. Early one foggy morning a fully loaded Mosquito fighter bomber with a two-man Australian crew hit some power lines beyond Whitwick pit away from Coalville, near where the present Community Hospital now stands. The explosion was heard miles away, scattering debris over five surrounding fields. The Home Guard mounted guard over the area and assisted in collecting up the live ammunition and debris. All the time there was apprehension with a fear of the unexpected, but Coalville was lucky and could have suffered much worse. Albert New ran a coal merchants business with his brother David from his farm at the bottom end of Owen Street. It was near here, by the Casseloid factory which was making Spitfire parts, that an unexploded monster bomb lay buried under his chicken run for nearly two years before it was defused. The bomb weighed in excess of 2,000lb. and if it had gone off would have flattened half of Coalville. It fell one Sunday night and many Coalville people heard the terrifying screaming whistle and waited with dread for the explosion that never came. As with the other bombs that were dropped on Coalville it was thought that it was released by a German bomber caught in the Altons searchlight beam, rather than that it was targeted on Coalville. When eventually this monster bomb was defused and dug out of its subterranean resting place, it was placed on display in the foyer of the Rex cinema, where people were encouraged to buy war stamps to stick on it in aid of the war effort.

Another incident occurred early one Easter Sunday morning when a German bomber released a stick of bombs which fell along the top of the Grange fields behind Snibston Colliery. One crater was near the bottom of the pit-bank (waste tip), just missing Snibston Lodge Farm, whilst another was in the field opposite Snibston school, the ones between lying along the farm road. More bombs fell in the London Road and Victoria Road areas, near Whitwick pit, and on the coal marshalling sidings at the back of Christ Church. Some of these were incendiary bombs and at least one of the other high explosive bombs, the one which fell near Whitwick pit, failed to detonate.

D-DAY AND BEYOND

As the winter months approached we were soon into 1944 and it was obvious that the invasion of Europe was soon to take place – everyone sensed it. D-Day (6th June 1944) came and went, our training went monotonously on, but it was from the autumn of that year that one particular day in my life in the Home Guard will always be remembered. It was a Sunday – destination unknown at the time – with orders for firing practice. As we 'bused into this firing range on the other side of the Six Hills cross roads, we realised it was no ordinary one. It consisted of 24 targets, the largest we had yet been on. Our orders for a start were to occupy the butts and record the scoring for those firing, and it was here that we discovered the difference from those earlier exercises. It turned out to be an American establishment – the Yanks had everything bigger and better than ours, or so it seemed. As we went up and down the targets, their names, their towns, their States were all cut out on the wooden beams and posts, all belonged to the 82nd American Airborne Division, just another name to us at the time, but history now shows it was one of their crack divisions. Our spell in the butts over, we had a few rounds of rifle fire ourselves then went on for a spell of machine-gun practice with the bren-gun. This was, or had been, the Regular Army's best light machine-gun; a few single shots to get the feel, followed by a short burst, was all that was allowed – you could soon get through some ammunition with this gun, and ammo was precious. What a change from the early days!

Just after our platoon had finished firing, the cease fire whistle went, and everyone was surprised. Surely they had not brought us all this way out for such a short exercise? This was the uncertainty which seemed to surround everything we did. So we played football to while away the time. Then the reason for our stand-down became obvious: with low-flying aeroplanes overhead we would have been a real hazard to their safety. First it was just a noise of planes in the sky, then it became a crescendo. We stopped playing, sat on the grass and witnessed an incredible sight: Dakotas loaded with paratroops towing gliders from Wymeswold airfield just beyond, so low they were only just missing the tree-tops. It seemed you could pluck them from the sky. I can only presume they were the American 82nd Division, for were we not occupying their vacated firing range. Whether it was them or the British Airborne Division I never found out, but whoever they were their training was over, and for many their lives also would soon be over. These events now have a place in history; it was the day British and American airborne divisions set off to secure the bridges over the river Rhine at Arnhem and elsewhere for the advancing Allied Armies. That day has an important place in my memory.

The winter months came and went and we were soon into the spring of 1945. With the war now going well men were drafted into the coal mines instead of the Armed Forces and everyone knew the end was drawing near. Men reaching call-up age were being given the option of military service or work in the coal mines. Many chose the mines, being known as Bevin Boys after the politician whose idea it was to supplement the hard pressed coal-face labour force with supporting drafted labour. Most of these got out after the war, although a few stayed on to make a career in the industry.

As the weather picked up in the early part of the year, orders came that all live ammunition was to be destroyed. One Sunday morning, before dismantling the bombing bay, the surplus hand grenades were primed and thrown for the last time. On another Sunday, the Molotov Cocktails were taken out of the dugout, lined up just like a shooting gallery to be destroyed by small-arms fire. This also used up the sten-gun ammunition. There was a great amount to destroy, but magazine after magazine were emptied before the task was completed. Some fired in anger, some in relief, but all knew a new life lay around the corner. They seemed far-off days since we had stood together to defend England with nothing but broom handles.

The Home Guard was a unique army. At its peak it mustered one and a half million men, all serving without pay. Many served with coastal anti-aircraft batteries and in other dangerous situations, and suffered high casualties. Some even received medals for heroism. I was 22 years old when the orders came that we were to be stood-down and disbanded. Looking back, I was proud to have done my bit for King and Country and was equally proud to have served with the men of "Dad's Army", for the quality of a man was not measured by the contents of his wallet, but in the man himself and his actions. In those dark days, ours was not to reason why; ours was to do or die! We had served our country well and despite the difficulties had acquitted ourselves with honour. We had also had some good times together.

Chapter Three

At New Lount Colliery

Just before my twentieth birthday in 1942, saw me leaving Snibston for New Lount Colliery where my father worked on the shaker-pan conveyors at the coal-face. This change gave me my first introduction to face work and its long-wall system (long, continuous coal-faces) of winning coal which was totally different from the stall work (short coal-faces, supported by pillars of coal) I had been used to.

My father, Bert, was born into a large mining family, at Penistone Street, Ibstock, in 1892. His three elder brothers were referred to by fellow miners as "Jack'o", "Jim'o" and "Tom'o". Bert retired in 1959 at the age of 67, having spent the whole of his 53-year working life in the coal mines. He married in 1911 and fathered nine children – five sons, all of whom were miners, and four daughters who themselves all married miners. We lived in Margaret Street, Coalville, near to Snibston Colliery, but Bert Woodward spent the last 32 years of his working life at New Lount.

I was put to work on a return airway, an underground roadway which carried the spent or contaminated air from the coal-face back to the surface. The return airway was supported by arches 9ft. wide by 8ft. high, which we called "rings", and the main gate loading point by arches 12ft. by 10ft.. As the face advanced, so these roadways had to be extended by blasting stone down to set the arch supports; this stone then had to be packed, or stemmed, into a space which was sometimes less than 2ft. high. The same work had to be done by another team in the main gate roadway that was at the other end of the coal-face and ran parallel with the return airway. I ached in every bone in my body during the first week on this job, but gradually the pains ceased as I got used to the work.

The word pit, used in the context of coal mining, refers to a series of connected workings in one or several seams of coal, and by this definition there were two pits at New Lount. Although 13 seams of coal were present, only four were worked – the Middle Lount, which was worked to within 60ft. of the surface, the Nether Lount, the Yard and the Lower Main, which split into two seams – the Upper Roaster and the Lower Roaster. The fireclay floor of the Yard seam was mined simultaneously with the coal until 1956 and was used at the Lount and Newbold pipeworks.

No.1 and No.2 shafts were sunk by the Leicestershire Colliery and Pipe Company in 1924-25 to the Yard seam, 120yds. below surface ground level. Coal turning officially commenced from both shafts in March 1925. No.2 shaft was deepened in 1933 to the Lower Main horizon at 150yds., where a new pit bottom was made. No.1 Pit contained the upper seams of coal, the Middle Lount and

Routine simulated accident practice at New Lount Colliery, about 1958. The N.C.B. ran centralised area ambulance depots, and each colliery had its own first-aid teams and trained ambulance men.

Nether Lount, whilst No.2 was an auxilliary, or jackie, pit as we called it, which worked the thin lower seams – Yard, Upper Roaster and Lower Roaster. The two pits were connected by underground roadways (passages).

During the early 1940s a gradual changeover to dip (inclined) workings was taking place and a steep (1 in 3) underground drift, connecting No.1 Pit to jackie pit, was completed at that time comprising 85 steps. In place of a hand-rail was an ordinary thick hemp rope for hanging on to; climbing those steps after a days work was no joke and was unavoidable. The old drift connecting the two shafts, which were at different levels underground, was the main emergency exit and water was continually draining into these existing roadways, often making them impassable. After the experience of wading through water up to your waist, we found it much more preferable to use the steps. Lount was also the shallowest pit in the coalfield, only 230yds. deep at its deepest point. Water would always find its way through the broken strata from the many ancient shafts and old workings in the coal seams above, which were worked in the seventeenth and eighteenth centuries, and which outcropped at the surface not far away.

Since nationalisation two drifts have been driven from the surface. The first in

The Snibston Colliery screening sheds, 1957. A general view of Snibston Colliery surface buildings, looking east from the pit bank, showing the Stephenson shaft headstocks and winding-engine house, with the main coal-picking shed in the foreground.

During the 1930s (and later until post-war reorganisation), raw coal was discharged straight from the tub tippler on to a slow-moving slat-conveyor. Best house-coal was picked off the belt and tightly stacked in wagons beneath the screening shed whilst the residue leaving the picking-belt was screened and graded by size. In those days, 'Snibston Best' large coal, 'London Nuts' and 'Kitchen Coal' were produced. There would have been about 30 'compensation men' employed on the screens and picking-belts. Working conditions were very bad, especially in winter.

1952-53 from the old Coleorton Colliery site down to the Yard seam level, to improve ventilation in the Middle Lount and Nether Lount seams. The second, driven in 1955 from the surface screening plant, was to carry run-of-mine coal and dirt and reduce manpower at the two winding shafts.

INITIATION

The Lower Roaster seam contained the best quality coal in the Leicestershire coalfield, but also contained a deadly amount of methane gas. During the third week

The Whitwick Colliery deep-seam screens, 1958. Inside the small-coal screening shed men are engaged in picking stone off the coal-grading conveyors. A middlings screen can be seen at bottom right. Cleaning the coal in this way was a very labour-intensive operation and a soul-destroying job for the men involved. These jobs disappeared with the introduction of modern coal-washing plants, as erected at Snibston in the late 1960s and where the combined outputs of Whitwick, South Leicester and Snibston Collieries were eventually concentrated.

at Lount and travelling the air-road on my own, I reached the point where we undressed, and put my shukie lamp on my cap. Then "whoosh!". The gas had ignited. My mates shouted "Get down, get down flat!" as the ignited gas sped towards them against the natural flow of air. Then came the explosion. The bang was terrific, I seemed left in a vacuum with no oxygen for a few seconds, until the natural air current took over, forcing the gases back over me down the air-road. Glancing up I saw the receding gas cloud contained all the colours of a rainbow. Men came rushing to me a few seconds later; all were astonished to find me uninjured except for a few slight burns on the neck. They said I was very lucky, and looking back I realise I was. This experience, especially the warning shouts, which had saved me proved invaluable in the next two or three years. It was the largest quantity of gas even the older miners had seen ignited. Afterwards, I was informed by the coal-fillers on the dayshift that the first thing they would do when going on shift, was to ignite their bore-holes and let them burn slowly like a candle to avoid any concentration. I had learnt my lesson the hard way and fully understood what they were telling me. After a few weeks, being deployed to work on my own, the same thing was to happen again, this time to a cockney man, Harry Fox, who had left London in the blitz with his family, then chose to work down the pits. This time I was to shout the same warning I had heard in my similar situation. His cockney accent plus the gratitude displayed when he realised what might have happened made a very funny ending to this incident. But, like me, he never forgot the lesson.

In late December 1942, after becoming more experienced in face work, I was deployed to work with my father and his mate Andy Rose advancing the steel shaker-pan conveyor which shook the coal along the coal-face on to a loading point in the main gate road. Each pan of the shaker-pan conveyor was approximately 10ft in length, and on a face of 120yds. required 36 or 37 individual pans. When these were fitted into their cradles the total height was barely 14ins. Steel ropes in 50yd sections were coupled together then fitted into clamps at each side of every pan. They were then tensioned up and secured by clamps on the tension pan to prevent them from parting.

Men at work on the picking belt of the South Leicester Colliery screens, 1960. Each colliery had its own often improvised screening system. After primary screening, lumps of stone were removed by hand and large coal was quality graded by the pickers.

Men at work on the picking belt of the South Leicester Colliery screens, 1960. Screen houses were very cold places and many men wore cheap but warm clothing from army surplus stores. The white armbands probably indicate old prisoner-of-war uniforms!

This was a hard job and not very rewarding; most days we left home at one-twenty in the afternoon to cycle to work, and such were the bad working conditions encountered that it was sometimes one, two or even three o'clock the next morning before we had returned the five miles home. Many an early morning we were stopped by Air Raid Wardens as they stepped out of the darkness with their "Put that light out!" But they soon got to know us and only really bothered us when German bombers were droning overhead. After working such long hard hours, there was only one place to be when we arrived home -bed (regardless of the planes!)

In Lount No.1 pit were found the thick coal seams of 4ft., 4ft. 6ins and 5ft.. This allowed coal-faces to adopt the endless belt conveyor system to carry away the coal to the loading point. Coal had to be shovelled on to the conveyor which stalled if it became overloaded. If the men continued loading the standing belt there was a danger of the belt breaking when an attempt was made to start it up again, and the outcome was an even longer stoppage. Money would be docked out of pay if any coal was left and men only received payment for the amount of coal they filled out, regardless of conveyor breakdowns. Standing time payment was not available in those days!. No.2 jackie pit, being a thin seam pit, had to have a much lower conveyor, hence the shaker-pans plus a bracket conveyor which used pans and chain. On a double-unit coal-face (two faces combined into one), there would be shaker pans on the left and a bracket conveyor (scraper chain) on the right. The bracket conveyor comprised a flat pan on the floor in which the underneath endless chain rode. A deeper, 9ins pan for the top chain transported the coal to a loading point, and into the coal tubs. On a double unit, approximately 25 men would be needed to complete the full extraction of coal.

THE UNION

Most miners, in those days, had little or no mathematical skill and were unable to work out the amount of wages due to them at the end of each week. This was based upon the tonnage filled out, number of shifts worked and the going rate per ton. I realised men were being done out of their rightful earnings after being asked to check the wages of a colleague. Irregularities were widespread and when I found I too was being cheated, I decided to attend Lodge Union meetings. After serving on the committee for a time I was elected chairman and schooled for this position by Bob Hatton, delegate, and Sammy Hutchinson, secretary. They were the best Lodge officials I encountered during my 45 years in the pits. Bob Hatton was relied upon many times to sort out grievances and see them put right, but he was disliked by some of his fellow delegates for his honesty and integrity.

In war time, even wild-cat strikes still arose through bad management and bad union representation. Old habits die hard! All pits were now working six days a week to supply coal to the hard pressed munitions factories and other industries involved in the war effort. But still, junior officials couldn't get out of the habit of cheating the workforce, and one particular incident involved our own Area Union Agent. The coal-cutter operators in jackie pit came out on strike over pay and we at branch level had the task of sorting it out. During our enquiries we were astonished at the lies this official conjured up to save himself and his position. He had done a dirty deal over the cutters' contract some years previously and was now trying to put the blame on two workmen. After we exposed his lies, he put a notice up stating, "Qwing to my lapse of memory there is no signed contract for jackie pit cutters". We considered this disgraceful behaviour. After a general meeting of all men at the pit, a vote of 'no confidence' was passed and the matter went before the Area Union Council, but their decision allowed this man to keep his position. The decision was to have serious repercussions a few years later and almost caused the breakup of the Union.

We at New Lount often wondered at the honesty and integrity of our Area Officials. It was not long afterwards that Frank Hodges, Managing Director, drew up plans for a consultation committee at Lount. Its object was to look at all aspects of the general running of the pit, including efficiency, production, and safety, but above all to bring a new spirit of working together and to develop practices which were acceptable to management and men. In Europe, I was to learn later, this was called participation. Here at last, through representation, men could air their grievances and channel their own ideas directly back to management; this was a great step forward in industrial relations. Frank Hodges was a national figure in the N.U.M. before going over to the management side, and was one of the major voices in the Union pressing for nationalisation of the coal industry immediately after the First World War (1914-18). Before working at Lount, his name was mentioned many times in our family home, always with respect. He knew how to get the best out of men and was not afraid to make hard decisions, but he was fair and honest with the workforce, so Lount Colliery was mainly a happy pit.

Shortly after the establishment of the consultative committee, I was again to witness the ignition of methane gases. One day my mate Andy crawled off the face into the return airway and as he stood up became engulfed in the ignited gas; as I dropped flat I shouted the same old warning, "Get down, get down!", and luckily he responded. It was a very strange experience indeed to keep finding myself in these situations. Sooner or later there would be a big bang – and dead men can't dig coal. Supported by union branch officials, the new consultation procedures gave us the opportunity to press for battery lamps to replace the naked light. Management conceded to our request since they too realised change was now necessary, and this gave more confidence on both sides. It must be stressed that ventilation in the pit was very good, but had it not been, there would have been many fatalities. Methane gas, being lighter than air, used to build up above the arch supports in every crack and crevice, the bigger the holes, the bigger the concentration. While on the subject of naked lights, I am reminded that miners smoked down the pits in those days, and Lount was no exception, but when we went over to battery lamps this gradually ceased as men realised the dangerous consequences of taking risks.

At Lount a concessionary coal allowance was in operation for all married miners, but to fund this, men at the coal-face were filling 21cwt. of coal to the ton. For every ton loaded out a hundredweight went back to management for administration of the scheme, so that some unmarried men on the big seams were conceding 20 tons a month.

Before the war New Lount colliery was a rather special pit for Leicestershire miners since the quality of coal made it easily saleable on the markets of the country. New Seam (jackie pit) coal was very shiny and bright and you really could call lumps "black diamonds", though it did contain the deadly methane gases already mentioned. It was this quality that kept the pit working, mostly four days a week during the summer months, providing miners with more work than any other in the coalfield.

PIT-HEAD BATHS

Lount Colliery was the first pit in the Leicestershire coalfield to have pit-head baths. This was way back in 1929 and despite early opposition when it was

The pithead baths at Snibston Colliery, 1942. These were opened on 30th October 1940. They stood opposite the colliery on the Ashby Road.

regarded as an impossible dream. There were many popular superstitions in the old days, such as, that too frequent washing of the back weakened the vital muscles, and that no one could wash the miners' back like his 'missus'. Sixpence per week were deducted out of my wages for this luxury and no miner begrudged it, for nothing was more refreshing than a nice hot shower and a change of clothes after a long shift in the pit. No longer was it necessary to trudge or cycle home in your pit dirt, and to have to wash away the black grime in a tin bath in front of the kitchen fire. Pit-head baths were a major step forward in the establishment of the miner's dignity and self respect.

Compressed air loading rams (mechanical pushing devices) were in operation at both pit-tops and pit-bottoms; these were installed by Westinghouse in 1937 and allowed one man (onsetter) instead of two to fulfil the task of despatching the coal tubs on and off the cages. It was still a very efficient system, even by 1942 standards. But there was always a problem in cold weather with freezing air lines, particularly in the downcast shaft, so to ease this hazard hot water was piped from the baths and run alongside the air pipes.

Snibston Colliery surface, 1957. The landsale area, with coal merchants and their lorries bagging and loading domestic coal in front of the loco sheds. Each merchant had his own waggon of coal and loaded his horse-drawn cart himself until motorised vehicles replaced them.

My father had related to me how the pit had, in its early years, been low on production and profitability, and with the old mining company going bankrupt the banks had brought in a South Wales Union man, Mr Frank Hodges, to rescue the ailing business. A new company was formed in 1933 and many new ideas introduced to drag New Lount into the twentieth century. Until then it was a very primitive concern, mostly on stall and pillar work with inadequate roadways. The new company immediately took over the old Coleorton Colliery ("Bug & Wink") on The Moor and, by ceasing production there, were able to transfer the output allocation to New Lount. This enabled them to increase production, and therefore profitability, at a time when colliery output was controlled by the Government. During my stay at Lount and after meeting Frank Hodges on numerous occasions, I had no doubts that he was the man who made the business tick. To get miners to work at Lount, which was roughly five miles from Coalville and four miles from Ashby, he introduced an attendance bonus, 2/6d a day, or in the war 15s for a full six days work. It was this incentive which made miners 'get on their bikes' and transfer to Lount, but if you lost a day's work you lost the whole 15s!

LONG WALL

By the time I went to work at Lount the pit operated the longwall system on all coal-faces with neither stalls nor ponies. They never had ponies at New Lount, but did have one at the Old Lount pit that closed in 1924 and stood by the Lount pipeworks, which in turn closed at the outbreak of war in 1939. Young men had to tram (push) the full coal-tubs 30 to 40yds. before they were hauled out by the haulage rope. We had to learn and adapt to all the new techniques before we could consider ourselves true miners. In those days you did not class yourself a miner until you could do most of the different coal-face jobs, and I was still under 21 years old. There was also a saying that once you had worked at Lount, you could work in any pit in the coalfield; from my experiences I must agree with this. It was also the most technologically advanced colliery of its day in the district.

I have already stated that I worked with my father on the shaker-pans which shook the coal to a loading point in the main-gate. The first coal being shovelled on the pans at the far end of the coal-face would be shaken a 100yds. or more along the face to its destination. The pans were made with a steel strip underneath which fitted into a slot in the conveyor cradle. Ball bearings allowed movement backwards and forwards and the drive came from an electrically powered machine in the pan-gate, situated about 16yds. up the coal-face. This was a specially prepared area in which the power machine had to be jacked up and wedged into the roof of the pan-gate to ensure no movement occurred during its operation. Reciprocating motion for the pans was created by rocker arms on the machine similar to the pistons in the engine room of a ship. To drag the pans about we had a steel hook similar to a fisherman's gaffe, plus a six pound hammer to set and remove roof supports. Clash, bang, wallop was the order of the day, hence the nickname which miners referred to Lount – "Clash". The hammer itself was always referred to as a "Lount spanner". To advance and assemble the pans in the new track required unity. One man lifted and another shoved to lip the pan over the one in front; at the other end the pan had to be lifted to slide the cradle under. Make a mistake and it meant busted fingers; with only 28ins of headroom it seems impossible that men were able to work in these conditions.

The jackie pit coal-cutters also had a strenuous job, though no job was easy. To make a little more height the cutter driver would cut in the dirt for two to two and a half inches, and this dirt had to be shovelled by the rest of the team over the pans into the gob (the waste area behind where the men were working). The first man at the back was the Banjo man; his job was to keep his shovel going to avoid the cutter getting clogged up and stalling. The next man also had to shovel like mad, whilst the third man, with a long flat shovel, would clean out the cut and place wooden blocks between floor and coal. He was the Gummer-out. Some names, but they fitted the job each man had to do! Last, but certainly not least important, the Cable man at the rear kept an eye on the cable and shovelled up the dirt that was left behind. So the coal-cutters required five men to cut the coal-face and prepare it for the coal-fillers on the day-shift. If this was not done efficiently it would make it harder for the fillers. On the day-shift itself the fillers were required to fill nine yards for their daily task. They would have wound in (drilled) one bore hole the previous day in preparation for firing, by means of a hand-operated worm drill, the support for which was provided by a notched wooden prop wedged between roof and floor. Miners were always very ingenious and inventive – they had to be. After firing, coal often jammed into the roof and had to be levered down, which was a very dangerous operation.

PAY PACKETS AND FOOD PARCELS

By now I was receiving my wages in a dignified manner as befits a self-respecting human being. Instead of the little tin with tally number on, containing money, we were now handed a proper wage packet. How our forefathers must have been humbled as they queued to receive their money thrown on to a table. Here at last the Second World War was bringing home the need for coal to refuel economic recovery, and gradually improvements in the miner's lot had to be introduced. Income tax was at a very high level in those war years, and for single men like myself it was a big blow to earning potential. Every year we received a statement on the over-taxed amount, which was to be redeemed in 'Post-War Credits', but it was some time after the war was over -in fact not until the mid 1950s – before the government of the day had the good grace to pay out.

1945 saw a change in the Union, when Leicestershire became an independent area within the National Union of Mine Workers and Frank Smith became Area General Secretary. Being detached from South Derbyshire, which also went its separate way, gave miners some financial reward from the disbursement of Union funds; so we Lodge officials had the happy task of paying out up to two pounds to miners who qualified with full years of service in the Union. Another rewarding task was helping to distribute surplus army ration boxes that the government had allocated to miners. Inside were tinned peaches, biscuits, thick Players cigarettes and a powdery kind of chocolate; these were indeed luxury items. Those who have lived through the war years will know what I mean after so many years of deprivation. On reflection, it is my opinion that the coal-owners of New Lount and other pits must have made extraordinary profits during the war, while miners were over-worked and under-paid, under-fed and over-taxed.

In May 1945, with the war coming to an end in Europe, things started to change for the worse. As the summer months rolled on, the owners of Lount Colliery brought in fresh management and Frank Hodges stepped down to spend more time on his farming activities at Smoyle Farm. It was soon apparent to Lodge Union officials that the good will established by the consultation procedures was a thing of the past. The iron rod was back, and to frustrate the Union, new management deployed our delegate and secretary to work night shifts instead of days. It was this attitude that decided me to leave New Lount and resume my working life elsewhere. The lifting of the essential work order gave miners the freedom of choice again, so I left in September 1945 for Bagworth colliery.

During the war, several changes in the immediate management of New Lount Colliery took place, particularly in 1939, 1940 and 1941, but the main control remained the same. In that period, outputs kept more or less rising to 1944 with an overall tonnage of over 548,000 tons of coal and 10,764 tons of clay. Output per manshift set up a new record of over 36cwt..

In 1947, New Lount produced 481,990 tons of coal with a labour force of 1,118 men and an average overall productivity of 36.5cwt. per man shift. In 1962 the output was 437,867 tons of coal with a labour force of 658 men and an average overall productivity of 58.2cwt. per man shift. In the week ending 16th December 1961, New Lount achieved its highest overall productivity of 66.4cwt. per man shift.

Chapter Four
The Bagworth Experience

With the ending of the war, a new revolution slowly began to unfold. It brought with it new men to work down the pits, and a new life for miners; a life that the men at "Snibby" had hoped and prayed for over many years. Little did we realise that this was the most important industrial and social change of the twentieth century for all coal-miners; gone were the days of working only two days a week, miners were now being asked to work six and seven days to help the country back on its feet.

Leaving Lount, which at that time operated the long-wall system on all its coal-faces, it was surprising to find that Bagworth still worked the stall system with ponies in one part of the pit. I joined a team of five men on a Middle Lount long-wall face 4ft. 6ins high. The six of us were responsible for moving the belt conveyor (120yds. long) into the new track, and packing in the old track-line, as the coal-face advanced. It was my first experience of belt conveyors and was very strange indeed working in much better conditions. One has to work in both the 2ft. 6ins and the 4ft. 6ins environments to appreciate the difference. This new system involved 8yds. by 4yds. packs with 6yds. of wastes between, and it was in this team that new ideas were successfully tried out to increase efficiency for doing the job. Little did we know that elsewhere, where the two jobs were not combined, the same task was requiring eight men. Packs were built up of stone, between the floor and the roof after the coal had been extracted, to support the overhead strata. It was not possible to replace the total support originally provided by the coal and the idea was to allow the roof to subside gradually behind the working area at the coal-face, thus relieving stress and cushioning the working area from the impact of settlement. The unsupported waste areas between the packs, which permitted the roof to collapse, provided the material for the packs.

Men were now being demobbed from the armed forces in increasing numbers, and much of this available man-power was absorbed into industry. It was no surprise that some of these men, from the city of Leicester and mostly with no mining experience, would seek work down the pits. Many of the experienced miners, who had worked in the pits throughout the war, were over 65 years of age and stayed on until they were 70. It was rumoured that one miner worked until he was almost 80. With the pressure on to increase coal production to meet the insatiable demand for fuel, the coal industry needed all the men it could get. One amusing incident springs to mind; a 30-year-old ex-soldier with wife and family in Leicester, on being demobbed from the army, was employed to work down the

Bagworth Colliery surface, about 1970. The right hand headstocks are for the top-seam upcast men and materials shaft. The left hand headstocks are for the bottom-seam downcast coal winding shaft.

pit. The first job assigned to him was to fetch a pony to get supplies in from the rope haulage. The ponies were used to the usual commands "Whoa boy!" or "Whoa Billy!", but the new man knew nothing of these. His military command "Halt!" was ignored by the pony, which casually turned its head in curiosity as it continued on its way. When the man did manage to wrestle the pony to a standstill he put the limbers on back to front, and the pony must have wondered whether it was supposed to be coming or going. After a good laugh two of us showed him the correct way, giving him a few tips on command, then the following day again showed him the correct procedure, assuring him the jokes and banter were not meant maliciously. His initiation was over, and when he too saw the funny side we became good friends. After this he began to talk freely about his war-time experiences and we were to learn what desert warfare was like.

NATIONALISATION

It was in 1947 after a long hard winter with roads blocked by snow-drifts 10ft. high that the coal industry was nationalised. Miners were put out on the streets to dig away the snow and restore communications between villages during this

The steam winding engine for Bagworth Bottom Seam, 1970, with its driver Fred Beeby. Throughout the coalfield these engines were kept in spotless condition and the warm smell of oil and steam was a special feature of the winder houses.

harsh winter. Nationalisation brought the five day working week – plus a week's holiday with pay – for the first time in history. This was a very important social change for miners and it allowed us to take a week's holiday like most of the other workers in the country enjoyed. This turned out to be very important to me, as along with friends we planned a camping holiday by the river Soar at the same location as the war-time Home Guard exercise. Here I met my wife-to-be, and we married the following year. She worked in a hosiery factory in Nottingham and had two weeks annual paid holiday.

Cruising down the river was a well known song of those years, so we too cruised down our own bit of the river; after six years of war and the tragedies it had brought we felt everyone had earned this new-found freedom. Although food was in short supply and still rationed (you needed coupons for nearly everything) the black market was very active, but if one had the money there was always a way around the coupon problem. Our camp was near the ferry at Zouch, on the river Soar. People wanting to cross from one side to the other would pull themselves over for a fee of one penny. The near-by farm kept us provided with a never-ending supply of milk, eggs and other produce. That summer of 1947 was fantastic and our holiday was the highlight of those balmy days, for we arose

The materials (top seam) pit bottom at Bagworth Colliery, 1980. A junction inbye showing fantail roof archwork.

with the sun and after a cuppa, took a dip in the river followed by breakfast, then lazing on the river bank and back in again for another swim. Many a time we went swimming in that river near midnight. What more could one ask? The social life at night was mostly going to the pictures or trying to find a public house that was open, as beer was still in short supply.

In that year even the pit ponies were brought up to the surface and put out to grass for a week. Before going off on our holiday I went up to a field near Snibston pit bank to renew old acquaintances with some of the ponies I had worked with at "Snibby". It was no use, they had gone completely wild again. From the days they had been captured on the moors of Dartmoor and Exmoor they had not known what it was like to feel the sun or rain on their backs, and I just sat and watched them enjoying their little bit of freedom before I too set off on my vacation.

Refreshed from the holiday it was back to work on the following Monday. In the next few years, although the pits were now nationalised, confrontation instead of conciliation always seemed to be the theme of management, encouraged, sad to say, by some union officials. In 1948, after nationalisation, we

The South Midlands Mines Rescue Team at Bagworth Colliery, 1985. Experienced underground workers were recruited from the collieries for special training as full-time rescuers. From their headquarters at Ashby-de-la-Zouch they were available immediately to respond to emergencies such as explosions, fires and roof falls. They covered the Leicestershire, South Derbyshire, Warwickshire and Kent coalfields.

too were to have a big scare. Riding the cages in and out the mine was a daily routine, but one day, coming up after our shift, we got to eye-level with the pit-top Banksman's feet, then the cage full of men suddenly plummeted what seemed like 30ft. or so back down the shaft, dangling there was like being on a piece of string ready to snap. It was a frightening experience! Reporting it made little difference as we were told it was imagination, but after several days of the same thing happening, to a lesser degree, we made it known we would not ride the shaft until the problem was rectified. Then we were told the difficulties had been caused by excessive slack in the winding rope after the fitting of a new rope, and at the weekend maintenance teams worked around the clock for two days to put matters right.

Knowing full well the extremes of poverty in previous years, miners were now to enjoy the benefits of prosperity, but the promise was slow to be fulfilled and the struggles to achieve it included the strikes of 1972 and 1974. By now, new heavier belt conveyors were being introduced as factories got back to producing goods for the home market. As we started installing these bigger conveyors, management still only wanted to pay the same rate as we were previously paid for moving the lighter structures, 8½d per yard, although colleagues were being

The Snibston Colliery pit ponies' holiday, 1954. Ponies at the Stephenson pit-top, brought to the surface for the duration of the annual holiday shutdown. The ostlers and shaftsmen are seen here holding the ponies whilst they get accustomed to daylight. In the background the headstocks of the tandem upcast shafts stand in front of the boiler-house chimney. The large hole in the front of the Stephenson steam winding engine house denotes the approaching end of the steam era, for the steam engine was replaced by electric winding machinery whilst the miners were away on holiday. In 1964 the upcast winder was also electrified.

paid 11d per yard over the border in South Derbyshire. By agreement, we had accepted all these new changes but management did not want to pay us for the heavier work. The union delegate was useless; his only concern was his own loss of wages during the discussions, but after strong bargaining by our team, we finally settled for 10d per yard.

One of the early initiatives in 1952 was the N.U.M.'s levy to supplement our old age pension at 65; we were asked to pay 6d per week and this was later increased to 1/6d, then to 3/4d. By the time I was made redundant in 1982, it had increased to 6.5% of my wages but our expectations have been sadly frustrated. This pension fund now has well over £5.5 billions. I have in my possession documentation of 1987 which led us to expect that all members still paying into

Snap time at Whitwick Colliery, 1958. "Lippers" J. Clarke, W. Johnson and N. Tebbit enjoying a few jokes at snap-time in the return air-road. Plastic water bottles (rear) were replacing glass bottles (foreground), and battery cap lamps were now being worn by all miners.

the fund, and beneficiaries drawing upon it, would each be credited with just over £52,000, which at the minimum expectation should yield a pension of £60 per week, but some ex-miners are still only receiving a mere pittance.

Everything began to alter dramatically now, for changes were accelerating on every front. During my stay at this colliery everything was tried to limit the damage caused by subsidence on the surface, which was very bad around Bagworth. Barlestone Row terraced houses at the top of the village suffered drastically and eventually the whole row had to be demolished. There was also great concern over the main railway line around Bagworth station where the line had to be lifted to maintain levels. From the conventional semi cave-in system, total cave-in (or crash-packing) was introduced in an attempt to reduce surface subsidence. Initially most of the theories put forward by the so-called experts were absolutely crazy and did not work on the Middle Lount faces, but the experience gained did improve miners attitudes to the changes which came later.

Crash-packing was not only crazy but bloody dangerous, and I must emphasise the adjective. This is where the packs, which cushioned the coal-face from total collapse, were removed and replaced by a long line of Walton steel chocks. The idea was that as these chocks were advanced daily there would be a total cave-in of the overlying strata behind the workings where the coal had been taken out, instead of being slowly cushioned by conventional packs. The first collapse brought the roof down with such a crash; one lump of rock measured 48yds. long, it was so big it was impossible to shine a lamp over the top of it. One wag christened it "The Vanguard" after the Royal Navy warship, and chalked up its name on the side. It was very nerve wracking from a working point of view. Eventually the principle was successfully applied after the introduction of hydraulic face supports, but at the time the idea was wrong with the equipment we had then. Bill Wardle, my workmate at that time was the most honest and dedicated man any employer could wish to have, but as he was nearing his sixtieth birthday these changes were having a profound effect on his health and we begged him to approach management for a change. After another short time off work he duly asked to be taken off the section. His replacement only stayed for about three months, then after serving his 14 days notice moved to South Leicester Colliery face.

Up and down the country the same sort of thing was happening and desperate necessity gave rise to great inventions as new ideas were tried out in every area of mining activity. As technology expanded, teamwork became essential. Many experts were involved, the expert miners at the coal-face, engineers who were asked to do impossible things, scientists with new materials and manufacturers who developed prototype machines. The days of the isolated miner working alone in his stall with a pick and shovel were over. But miners still maintained it was the men on the coal-faces who were the real experts, for a coal-face is like a woman, the more you lived with her the more you knew her. So, throughout my mining career the coal-face was always referred to as "she".

A floor-heave in an underground roadway at the 71's supply-gate roadway, Snibston Colliery, 1981. This severe deterioration is due mainly to floor lift. Pressure from the surrounding strata has caused the floor to heave up into the roadway void, though a small amount of roof fall can also be observed. Note the Davy lamp which emphasises the extent of the damage, and the electric power cable snaking its way through the devastated area.

Among the real experts were the coal fillers; they were required to fill 8 yds. or 9 yds. of coal (a "ratch") according to each man's capability, and of course they were paid proportionately. Each man was responsible for maintaining high efficiency in roof control and was required to set his supports (pit props) within guidelines laid down by established rules. The Deputies, underground officials responsible for the safety of everyone working underground, made sure no one stepped out of line, and everyone worked in close harmony in their common interest. To set arch supports was skilled work of another kind and involved blasting and ripping main-gate and supply-gate stone lips. The lip is the edge or rim of the strata left after the daily advance of the coal-face. These men were known as main gate lippers and air-road lippers; they knew where to drill bore-holes to perfection and this was an art as well as a science which took many years to perfect. Coal and stone headings (tunnels) were a different matter; men who worked on these jobs had the knowledge and experience for blasting, ripping and

Snibston Colliery surface, after reconstruction, 1973. In the sidings are 32-ton hopper-bottom "merry-go-round" wagons and behind these is the new coal preparation plant. To the right are the air casings and axial mine ventilating fans on the tandem upcast shaft headstocks.

filling the material, driving a coal-cutter, setting arch-supports and extending their own conveyor -a combination of all the skilled jobs.

When at a later date mechanisation brought into the pits huge machines – D.R.C.L.s, J.C.M.s and Dint-Headers – to eliminate most of these manual jobs, progress was speeded up. Miners could now advance their heading from 2 yds. or 3yds. per day, up to 10, and even 14yds. It was the age of the new-style modern miner. Men went along with the new changes and, by trial and error, adapted working practices to succeed in this new machine age. Miners entering the industry in the 1970s were now trained by these 'old hands' who had had to learn the hard way.

By this time conditions began to get really bad. The Middle Lount seam was always worked at 4½ft.; over that height there was 6ins of "scud" – a mixture of coal and stone but black, which if left alone was bonded to the stone above and created good working conditions. Management had this band mined along with the coal for production purposes and this caused havoc, for air could get into the breaks and crevices in the stone which were weaknesses of the roof. The roof would then begin to break up and extra supports had to be set to counter this and secure the coal-face. The need for a good roof was essential for one's own safety. Older miners would always insist to younger men "Keep your back safe ma'lad" – in other words "Watch the roof, your life is at stake". They taught us how to 'sound' the strata by rapping on the roof with a pick or hammer. With experience you could tell if the strata had parted just above the coal by a hollow sound. If in any doubt you would try again and again until you were certain the roof was sound, for 'mother nature' acted very peculiarly at times. In emergencies, where the roof had caved in, miners would often transmit signals through to men on the other side of the fall by rapping on the coal-seam, awaiting a reply by the same means from those in danger.

Crash-packing in the Middle Lount seam added to the dirt content of the raw coal coming out of the mine; for Bagworth was also working a split Nether Lount seam, where a 10ins dirt band ran through the coal and was not separated cleanly at the coal-face. It was not until many complaints arrived from the power stations about high ash content that something was done about the problem. Then the need for better screening plant on the surface led to new techniques in coal preparation and blending being adopted. Awareness at the coal-face for producing clean coal became important for everyone, particularly the coal fillers, with daily output figures and saleable tonnages published on the pit-top. Quality control became a very big issue and at a later date saw the need for quality control officials underground.

DISSATISFACTION

The low rates of pay at this time generated a lot of bad feeling and were a very unsettling factor in our day-to-day working life. On the night-shift we were required, between 10.20 pm and 3.45 am the next morning, to fill the coal and stone left by the previous shift, and for this we earned the derisory sum of 15s, with no one to turn to for justice. Being family men with financial responsibilities it became obvious it was time to leave Bagworth. During the second week of my two weeks notice, abnormal working conditions allowed me to earn £8-7s-4d for a full week's pay, and this was in 1956. At this time, day-wage men at Bagworth were getting over £11 per week and miners' daughters working in the hosiery industry in Leicester were earning between £38 and £40 per week. By moving to a near-by colliery, I was able to lift my earnings to over £18 during my first week.

But moving jobs was not straightforward, for I found that an order had been given to colliery management in the Area not to set on miners from other pits. After 19 years working in the industry, and surviving all the changes which had taken place, freedom of choice as to where I could work was denied me; together with others who had taken the same action we found ourselves out of work. The Wednesday following I sought out Mr Johnson, the manager of Ellistown Colliery, for a job. He had been our manager previously at Bagworth; not only was he a good manager, he was a real miner and he knew his men. Despite the order, he gave a job to all of our team who wanted to continue in the pits. Not all did of course, and two of our team who lived in Leicester sought work elsewhere, outside the industry. Starting back to work, on the pit 'bus I was to meet Bill Wardle my old work-mate from Bagworth. He explained he was being forced back on the job vacated by our departure, but looking for him on the 'bus next day I found he was missing. Before going to work Tuesday night I was told he had said goodnight to his wife, then instead of going to work had gone down the hedge-side of a field and hanged himself. I was sickened and saddened by the news of having lost a good friend and workmate, but the N.C.B. had lost the most honest and dedicated workman I ever worked with during my 45 years in the coal mines. In their lust for position and power, some management showed no compassion towards the elderly miners who had been pillars of the coal industry.

Chapter Five
A Final Move to Ellistown

I started back in work at Ellistown Colliery in February 1956, this time on a High Main coal seam 4ft. to 4ft. 6ins high; back again on the semi cave-in system of packs and wastes instead of the crazy crash-packing which had previously scared the life out of us. This seam of coal had different characteristics not encountered before, for when the strata in the waste area collapsed it would pour out just like sand. As at the other pits, we had a lot of unskilled men employed underground at Ellistown and it was usual for them to be working with experienced colleagues. But this was not always possible. A few weeks went by, then to the alarm of everyone, the danger cry "Come on!" was heard and we all rushed forward to free a new man buried up to his neck. While we frantically fought to extract him, keeping his head from being submerged by the cascading debris, we feared for his mate who was nowhere to be seen and thought he was completely buried. It was soon learnt that he was also a new man and had panicked and run. Experienced miners didn't run away from mates in danger, they ran to them, as I had already found out in my earlier years at the coal-face. However, most miners were sympathetic towards unskilled men in these circumstances, especially when two were working together. Having freed the man we found his injuries were not of a serious nature and he was suffering mostly from shock, but he never returned to this job again.

In midsummer of that year, again with my mates, our lives were threatened from an unexpected source. It was on the afternoon shift sometime between four and five o'clock that the earth all around us really moved. The steel props supporting the roof shook and quivered like none of us had seen before. It was very frightening for a few seconds, then suddenly it ceased. Not knowing what had happened and thinking that perhaps there had been an explosion in another part of the pit we made our way to the nearest telephone in the return air road, to be informed from the surface that we had had an earthquake. Being reassured we went back to work to continue our shift, but arriving home that evening my wife recounted what had happened in the house: windows rattled, cups and saucers shook in the cupboards and plaster was torn away from the walls and ceiling in the bedroom. The record will show that it was only a minor tremor but 'mother earth' had really shaken the houses, and we had been over 800ft inside her when it happened.

In 1958 I was again deployed on another low coal seam, the Yard, and once more conditions were so bad that new ideas and initiatives were needed to work

The office block of Ellistown Mine, 1971. Behind the lorry can be seen the access tunnel to the colliery yard.

the coal efficiently. Sometimes working space was down to 19ins and it was impossible to swing a shovel. Fortunately the manager was aware of developments at other pits where these conditions prevailed and discussions took place with us to see if we could apply these methods at Ellistown. We were all of one mind for once, and as men and management worked together the coal-face was revitalised. But gradually the old jealousies between officials and other workmen came up again. I was to find out from this experience that some men, officials included, were afraid of change, they were sceptical of any new ideas. Little did they know that greater changes in the coal mines were about to overtake us all.

MECHANISATION

Up to this point in my working life there had been much of the traditional atmosphere underground, and although we had indeed seen many changes in working practices since my early days at Snibston, things had altered gradually. But now, at Ellistown during 1958 and 1959, as elsewhere in other coal mines

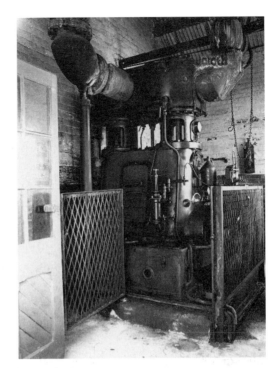

The Bellis & Morcom steam engine at Ellistown Colliery's fan house, 1978. This drove a Walkers stand-by fan prior to the electrification of the main fan. When this new main fan was installed the Walkers fan and all its associated equipment and buildings were demolished and the old main fan became the stand-by.

The screening plant at Ellistown Colliery before surface reorganisation, 1971. On the left is the landsale weigh-office and on the right are the outloading bunkers for lorries. In front runs Victoria Road.

Miners waiting to ride the shaft at the start of their shift at Desford Colliery's No. 1 downcast pit top, 1958. In the centre the banksman is releasing a full tub of coal from the pit cage which hangs from suspension chains. Men had to wait for coal winding to cease when they were wound in coalturning shafts, but usually they travelled in the upcast shaft which was used for materials and men.

Cutting a main-gate roadway, Snibston Colliery, 1980. This Dosco Roadway (Mk IIA) Cutter-loader, has just struck a fault in the 72's Main-gate roadway on the New Main coal-seam. Here stone has suddenly replaced the coal. The ventilation air-ducting (trowing) delivers fresh air into the heading and disperses the dust-contaminated air when the machine is working. Corrugated sheeting and mesh can be seen between the newly-set arches to prevent fall-out of loose stone.

up and down the country, the great Mechanisation Revolution was beginning. This was to be the new age of monster machines and vast capital expenditure; the industry was on the threshold of changing from being 'manpower intensive' to 'capital intensive'. Panzers, the name of German armoured weapons in the war, now became the name of armoured conveyors on all coal-faces. Trepanners, Tre-Pan Shearers, and single and double ended Shearers were just some of the names of these great machines which operated on the Panzers at increasing cutting speeds. The early coal cutting machines would strip (cut) and load coal on to the armoured conveyors at up to 10ft. a minute, regardless of the thickness of the seam, and were hauled along the coal-face by means of the dreaded haulage chain, detested by all in the coal cutting team because of the dangers this heavy chain presented.

It was about this time also that the industry converted to metrication and we were required to start thinking in terms of millimetres, centimetres and metres instead of inches, feet and yards. Team-work became more important than ever before, for everyone was now dependent upon the machine for their wages, and gradually all men came to accept this fact. New techniques required to work the system efficiently were introduced by members of the team and gradually this team spirit began to pay off. But the more successful we became, confrontations developed with management who seemed determined to cheat us out of the benefits we had rightfully earned. Method Study arrived at the coal-face and norms became the thing of the day, which were often used without any sense or reason and bore no resemblance to normality at all. Teaming up with Reg Hemsley, a man of principle with high ideals, I was persuaded in 1960 to join the N.U.M. Lodge Committee at the pit. From then on we both endeavoured to establish realistic norms with our overseers. Although this was to have been to everyone's advantage, with increased productivity and wages, there were continuing obstacles placed in our way, often from unexpected sources, which meant that many good ideas were killed stone dead before they were even considered. On the other hand, manufacturers were quick off the mark and were always ready to listen to any practical suggestions put forward by men on the coal-face. Private industries making mining equipment were now competing more than ever with their rivals to secure the many lucrative contracts offered by the expansion of mechanised mining. Dowty Engineering had the right approach and their willingness to listen to the men who actually used their equipment was reflected in the early improvement and rapid development of the Dowty hydraulic powered roof supports.

By now we had a mechanisation overman, Jack Robinson, who bore the brunt of all this new technology. He had plenty of good ideas of his own and the wisdom to listen to the theories of others. In choosing the most practical solutions and applying himself to see that they worked, Ellistown Colliery was kept going in these difficult years, at a time when production could have ground to a standstill. Coal mining in this country has moved a great step forward since those early days, but the foundations of modern mining methods were built on the shoulders of men like Jack Robinson.

HEADINGS AND TUNNELLING

After working on two mechanised coal-faces, and as the pressures for more development work grew, Reg and I became involved in driving roadways (tunnels) and opening up new coal-faces. The old coal cutting machines, which had served the mining industry well over the years, were now being taken out of service and headings in solid stone, coal and a combination of both were driven by blasting. Here again, new techniques had to be developed and perfected using explosives as efficiently as possible. These explosives had to be accounted for and were collected from the powder store at the beginning of the shift. Twenty pounds of the stuff had to be carried, slung around your neck, to meet the needs of the day. Once

An underground roadway at Ellistown Colliery, 1975. This roadway serving 63's coal-face is constructed with flat topped arches instead of the traditional steel arches or half-rings. Known down the pit as Hush Puppies (because we could not get our tongues around the German name of their manufacturer), these flat topped arches have pivotted joints which allow better settlement to strata pressure, and give extra width to the roadway without excessive height. The roadway was driven with a Joy Continuous Miner Mk II machine and has track for the Becorit haulage locomotive in addition to the belt conveyor. Coal is carried out of the mine on the conveyor system and materials required to service the coal-face are taken in by the Becorit train. Where long distances are involved between the pit-bottom and the coal-face men are transported in both directions by specially adapted manriding trains. The Becorit system, by which the locos and carriages were captivated inside the flanges of the track, allowed small locomotives to get supplies inbye in much faster time. The bright light (centre distance) is on an approaching train.

blasted down, the material had to be loaded out onto a take-away conveyor by shovel; but this was a slow business before Joy loaders were introduced to mechanise the operation. Being small and very manoeuvrable this machine was really effective. M.C.3s followed for the larger road-ways and greatly improved advance rates were achieved with these new machines. Competition between manufacturers in this particular field became very keen and this went a long way in pushing along engineering development of the later road-heading machines.

The Ellistown 63's coal-face, 1976. This photograph shows the Nucleonic probe which controls the steering device on the coal-cutting machine. The probe senses the thickness of the roof coal and allows a consistent layer to be maintained for operational and safety reasons. On the left is a clear view of the long-wall coal-face shows where the strip of coal has just been cut, and the regular marks of the disc-mounted cutter picks which are obscured by the probe and its supporting structure. Bottom centre, the Panzer, or armoured face conveyor can be seen, with the tubular captivation rail for the machine to the right of the scraper chain. The heavy duty haulage chain at bottom right runs parallel with the AFC and the Bretby power-cable carrier which can be seen behind the chain. Overhead are the hydraulic roof supports with cantilevers extended, protecting the 'new' roof prior to advancing AFC and roof supports over to the coal-face.

With Reg, Johnnie Hunt, Dickie Davis and Ivan Bills, we drove the North Return Air-road using a Joy loader; the same team also drove the first coal-face at Ellistown which extended the face Panzer as it advanced. This system was adapted on all subsequent faces into stable-holing. Here an area was prepared at each end of the coal-face for the massive coal cutting machine to enter so it could be prepared for its return journey back down the face. Then in 1968/69 the five of us, with Frank Matchett, in two teams of three, using D.R.C.L. machines, were involved in driving an underground connecting roadway between Ellistown and Bagworth workings, with Bagworth teams tunnelling from the opposite direction. Until the colliery ceased production in 1989, this tunnel carried all the run-of-mine coal away from Ellistown. Although it was called the Bagworth Trunk Conveyor the output from both collieries was conveyed underground to the Nailstone Drift Conveyor, thence to the surface and into a new coal preparation plant at the old Nailstone Colliery site. After this, I went to work on the south side of the pit in a J.C.M. (Joy Continuous Miner) team. This machine was the most flexible of all I had worked with. Just in one seven and a quarter hour shift the team advanced 16yds. and as far as I know this rate was not bettered in Leicestershire. It was achieved by close team-work, each man working together as a single unit. My work mates were Tony Bell, Teddy Harris, Brian Roleston, Dougie Walker, and Billy and "Lonza" Freeman.

TRADE UNION EDUCATION

At Ellistown we supported the Retired Miners and Widows Concessionary Coal Scheme, pioneered by a group of miners at Whitwick Colliery back in 1955, with George Ward and D.Roomes as its main architects. Taking up an interest again in Trade Union activities gave me a voice in the area union and provided the platform to support this scheme which provided for a better quality of life after retirement. Administered by the N.C.B., the scheme saw both sides – management and unions – slowly coming closer together on this one important issue. Men had been asked to give back 10cwt. of their concessionary coal allowance to a pool, which provided four loads of coal to retired miners and their widows. At the beginning the scheme ran into difficulties through a combination of inadequate contributions and financial problems. It needed a collective agreement from the other pits in the scheme to agree any changes, particularly the need for more contributions from the workforce. My personal feelings were that miners could now get by on 10 tons per year instead of the original 12, as much of the heating and cooking, once accomplished by coal fires, was now being done by gas and the new electrical appliances coming into the home. This bold initiative in Leicestershire succeeded, to the credit of all concerned.

Serving the union gave one a voice on the internal running of the pit, in such things as agreements on working conditions, establishing 'norms' or drawing up contracts. With the introduction of mechanisation and the hazards attendant upon powerful machinery in confined spaces, safety in the industry became a paramount issue. The N.U.M. set up site and accident inspectors to represent men seeking industrial injury compensation claims. Consultation between management and unions was introduced by the setting up of Colliery and Area Consultative Committees, at which all departments of the pit had a say in matters of safety. Area and Regional specialists were encouraged to present aspects of their work on such topics as industrial disease, dust control, ventilation and underground explosions. The N.C.B. Research Establishment at Buxton,

Derbyshire, gave an insight into the causes and nature of explosions and stressed the need for union representatives to get the message across to all concerned, of how easy it was to cause an explosion and loss of life. In an area where there was a high concentration of methane gas, even a bit of silver paper from a chocolate wrapping, or a small piece of aluminium lying about on the floor, if struck by a piece of steel, could cause the hot spark needed to set off a fatal explosion. Visiting the Buxton test site just after the Cresswell Colliery explosion where miners lost their lives, we saw a simulated re-enactment of this disaster under controlled conditions and it was brought home to us how easy the same fate could befall anyone who neglected the basic safety rules.

Through the N.U.M. and its affiliation with the National Council of Labour Colleges I was sponsored, in 1963, to attend summer school in Basle, Switzerland, and on 28th June departed with two other local colleagues, all expenses paid, including reimbursement of lost wages and with twenty pounds pocket money. It was my first time out of the country but the departure was memorable for another reason: after waiting in the terminal building at Gatwick airport that Saturday night, we learned that our flight had been delayed to give precedence to an incoming aeroplane which carried President John F.Kennedy on a visit to England. Assassinated in the following November, Kennedy was a popular man of those times and his death shocked the world. Though being away for only a week, I was grateful for the opportunity to broaden my knowledge of world affairs. The lectures dealt with the International Labour Organisation (I.L.O.), the Common Market (Britain was in E.F.T.A. at the time), trade union history and many other interesting topics. Then we had a most enlightening factory visit. This factory in central Switzerland was fully automated and had a very effective worker participation system which we discussed with management. The workforce elected the most intelligent of their number to represent them on the board of management, made up of 51% management and 49% workforce, and this team was responsible for running the factory. They held regular meetings to discuss operational efficiency, profits, dividends and investment; pay rises often came bottom of the list of priorities, as without a profitable business there were no jobs. They could override any trade union official with a grievance, or nip a wild cat strike in the bud if necessary to ensure the wheels kept turning, and disputes were always sorted out before they got to the confrontation stage. Centralised agreements were negotiated in a friendly and constructive atmosphere and were mainly adopted as policy by the trade unions without dissent. This experience was to change my outlook in many respects. Women did not have the right to vote but nevertheless exercised their influence by organising themselves together to petition Parliament.

On a balcony overlooking the river Rhine, our party was wined and dined by courtesy of the Basle Town Council, thus concluding a successful and very enjoyable week. The visit to the factory convinced me that participation was far better than confrontation, both for employers and employees.

At this time in Leicestershire, before a national pay structure was introduced in 1966, agreements on pay were negotiated by each pit and I considered this to be very unsatisfactory, especially in the case of heading contracts. Elsewhere, agreements negotiated for mechanised operations boosted earnings, but not being quite in this category, Ellistown 'pick & shovel' men did not receive these benefits. So I put forward a recommendation at our branch meeting proposing that we should seek centralised agreements, but this was defeated. The matter was brought up at the following meeting, when I pointed out the unfairness of the system which was operating at Ellistown, to our disadvantage. Again, I received no support. By being one of the last pits in the area to be fully mechanised, Ellistown colliery was not in an advantageous position when it came to negotiating rates of pay, and current arrangements at branch level needed to be addressed in a more constructive manner.

The following year 1964 I received an invitation to attend Ruskin College, Oxford, for a week. On the agenda was the next five years planning for the nationalised energy industries, coal, gas and electricity. Books and other literature arriving at my home gave all the background information, and it was fascinating to read how European countries were subsidising their own energy industries, especially coal. Out of four major countries – Belgium, France, Germany and the United Kingdom, Belgium came top of the list with U.K. at the bottom. These were the great issues being addressed and whilst I acknowledged their wider implications to the coal industry union representatives, I felt more concerned with local issues, and therefore declined the invitation.

In 1966 another setback to skilled miners and their families was forced upon us. The National Coal Board and the National Union of Mineworkers jointly introduced a new national pay structure. Its object was to close the gap between the highest paid and the lower paid workers; my wages dropped from £37-10s per week to £25, which was the top rate of pay for all skilled workers. Ironically, this 'brilliant' strategy did close the gap but did nothing for those on the low rate. In my opinion this imposition was the beginning of the long period of confrontation which led up to the 1972 seven-week strike. Although new and better machines were being introduced the earning potential at the coal-face had been eroded. Our area union supported the pay-grade structure against an undercurrent of resentment, and with others I was at pains to point out the anomalies in this agreement. The Leicestershire coalfield had one of the highest levels of productivity in the country, yet it finished up joint lowest on the pay grades. During the following six years miners began to leave the pits for better conditions elsewhere. In 1971 wages up to £45 a week were not unusual, against £29 in the pits. All the previous goodwill and willing effort by Leicestershire miners since the ending of the war counted for nothing. For those like myself with specialised mining skills, who had been in the industry all their lives, it was too late to learn new trades and we had no option but to stay on in the pits and grin and bear it.

THE 1972 STRIKE

In 1971, with worsening relationships in the industry, the nation's miners gave their National Union leaders a mandate to call a strike if negotiations with the National Coal Board failed to win an improvement in pay. These discussions failed and we were called out on strike 9th January 1972, the first such action since 1926. It was now our turn to experience the deprivation and bitterness of industrial action over a period of seven weeks. Although Leicestershire miners had voted with a small majority against the strike, they nevertheless came out in support of the national call, since everyone was conscious of the adverse pay differential with other major industries. It had not helped matters when sub-contractors, brought into one of the other pits in the area, were being paid £91 a week against our £29, particularly as some miners were doing nearly twice the amount of work.

During the strike, we had to resort to desperate measures to keep our families fed and warm and had no option but to go into the woods for firewood. I was very saddened by all this unnecessary suffering; it just didn't make sense. Here was I in the same situation my father had been in 46 years earlier, but this time we were a Nationalised industry. No longer could we blame mercenary coal-owners for our wretchedness. The industry was now owned by the nation and run by the people for the people. Where had we gone wrong? Did the country want coal; did they in fact want miners? Like the fighting forces during the war, we had given all we had and now there was nothing more to give. One miner summed it up: "They want you to work for them but don't want to feed you".

The seven week dispute was also a test for relationships within the family where the women had to carry the heaviest burden. They seldom complained and outshone their menfolk in fortitude and determination. It was this support that gave us the will to see the struggle through to the end, when, after seven weeks of dispute the Arbitration Courts judged in favour of the miners. So it took seven weeks to restore some of the disparity which existed between miners and workers in other industries. Leicestershire miners also gained parity with those areas such as Nottinghamshire who had been on £1 per day more; but the fight had been a bitter one, and on return to work there was an undercurrent of distrust and resentment which simmered on in men's minds, and which eventually gave rise to further disputes.On reflection of the strike itself, I am saddened at our area union's incompetence in handling this dispute. My own social security entitlements amounted to nothing since such payments as were due went directly to the wives and children. The first social security payment my wife received at the beginning of the strike seemed inadequate, so I went to inquire at the Miners Welfare Club, which had been taken over by Social Security and an army of civil servants, to deal with Leicestershire and South Derbyshire Area claims. The civil servant that dealt with my complaint worked it out and informed me that my wife was being underpaid. He said he would make sure the matter was put right but the following week nothing had been done about it, so I protested again. The same gentleman informed me his figures were correct and confirmed my own calculations were accurate. He went to discuss it with the supervisor, but she would not accept his findings. My request to see the supervisor was declined and I had to await an opportunity to confront her in full view of her staff, when it was necessary to complain about the running of the whole social security operation. After sitting down with two other members of her staff she conceded that we were right. This business took six weeks to rectify, but eventually my wife's entitlements were fully restored. Most men had been treated in this vindictive manner and I blame our area unions for this charade, and the incompetent handling of the dispute, which left miners more bitter than before. Especially sad was the fact that this bitterness set one miner against another, and the responsibility for this I lay at the door of the union.

During this time we gave up our beer and cigarettes, and I have never smoked since; we even had to stop buying newspapers and making payments on our life insurance policies. For single men the hardship was even greater, as no payments, either from social security or union funds, were made to striking miners. They had to take part-time jobs wherever work could be found, such as delivering free newspapers, or rely on charity. Life was very bleak for everyone.

BACK TO WORK AND TROUBLED WAT

Working to produce coal again recommenced, very much   but initially the extra money in our pay-packets made little differe   standard of living, for what it had cost us to achieve this improvem   months and more to recover. By this time, earlier rumblings of discon   beginning to boil up into confrontations with management and sign   next strike were looming on the horizon. Government policy had enc   schools, hospitals and factories to switch to oil for heating and industrial process   price of oil from the Middle East had been kept artificially low   pressures, but during 1973 the Arabs initiated price increases   crude oil to more than double its price at the beginning of   urn put pressure on the economy.

From 1st November 1973 with deteriorating wo   miners again voted for a ban on overtime, and three days later the Prime Minister announced, on radio and television, that the country had been p   National Emergency as a result of an impending fuel crisis. It   miners! How idiotic this sounded to me. Leicestershire miners   ve day week producing coal, and their only 'threat' was   hour-a-day voluntary overtime. Up to this point in my life, t   National Emergencies, the Second World War, the Suez Crisis   now this

During the winter of 1973, factories were put on   week as the political climate worsened. Christmas, normally   good

Underground manriding haulage at South Leicester Colliery, 1976. The miners are riding in open, rope-hauled cars. Ellistown Colliery used the Becorit monorail system.

will was marred by power cuts and shortages. Electricity cuts and black-outs now became regular occurrences in many homes, partly reminiscent of the war years. The ordinary working miner felt powerless and helpless in this ongoing conflict; would we never be given the respect that is the right of every human being, would we ever be treated fairly? How could we help but compare our lot with our neighbours? A person living close to me, working in a factory for three days on short time and getting three days dole money, was £1 per week better off than me working five days and getting one bonus-day payment.

The media were masters at exploiting situations for their own ends, often stirring things up out of all proportion to get 'good' copy, and on television our union Area Secretary entered the fray and dropped a monumental clanger. The National Union of Mineworkers had balloted all members to call an overtime ban beginning 1st November 1973. Leicestershire miners, along with other areas voted on the issue, but by a slight majority went against the national trend. Nevertheless, by accepting the national verdict for an overtime ban, Leicestershire remained solidly behind the N.U.M. Executive and had been operating the ban for a number of weeks. Our Area Secretary then invited television into his home where the interviewer asked the question: "In view of an impending national coal strike, does this vote mean Leicestershire miners would not come out on strike?"

Had he made it clear that his comments were his personal assessment of the mood of the men he represented, then things would not have got out of hand. However, his answer was an authoritative statement that Leicestershire miners would not come out on strike. He was seen on national T.V. news, and his comments heard by the general public as far away as the Isle of Wight. "Leicestershire miners would disobey any national strike call". Sitting in my lounge that Sunday night I was astounded by his comments which flew in the face of Trade Union democracy and unity. For this action miners were to condemn him; he had done nothing to help our cause. But "Joe Public", in the person of a little old lady from the Isle of Wight, was reassured and sang his praises on a follow-up programme.

On Monday morning, men at various pits in the area discussed the situation arising from this incident; a lot of questions needed answering, for it was seen as a betrayal of loyalty to his own men and the union in general. It was not until we heard that some pits had stopped work and walked out in protest, that we at

Driving a roadway in the New Main seam at Snibston Colliery, 1980. Here Colliery Overman Jack King (left) and a colleague stand next to a Dosco Dint Header.

The Chairman and the collier at Bagworth Colliery, 1973. On the left is Sir Derek Ezra, Chairman of the National Coal Board. He is chatting to coal-face worker Ronnie Oliver during snap time while on a visit to the colliery.

Ellistown made the same decision and came out with them. At a special area council meeting, a vote of 'no confidence' in the Area Secretary was tabled and carried, followed by a mass meeting of all miners in the area. This combination of events decided Leicestershire miners, on Thursday 31st January 1974, to vote for a strike, the first time in their history.

THE 1974 STRIKE
TRADE UNION ACTIVITY ON THE PICKET LINE

The 1974 strike was to last four weeks, and being a member of the local lodge committee, I found myself on the Ellistown picket line from day one. I started at 5.45 am on that first Saturday morning and also on every other day during the rest of those cold February mornings. The area union's policy was only to picket the place of work, in our case Ellistown Colliery, and only branch union officials to be present on the picket line. No secondary picketing was contemplated. It was also policy that only the Branch Secretary would have any verbal contact with any colliery official crossing the picket line. As in most industries, so within the N.C.B., different sections of the workforce were represented by different unions.

We in the N.U.M. were the skilled miners and labourers, and it was left to us, yet again, to carry the burdens of industrial action in pursuit of a fair wage for all.

The management union (British Association of Colliery Managers) and the colliery officials union (National Association of Colliery Overmen, Deputies and Shotfirers) were not bound in any legal sense by our strike action, but we felt that the officials, at least, with whom we worked in close daily contact had a moral obligation to support our cause, from which they also would benefit financially. So as the N.A.C.O.D.S. men arrived for work that first day of the strike, our Lodge Secretary addressed them from the picket line: "This is an N.U.M. picket line, we are asking for your support; we are asking you to turn back and not enter the colliery". Our orders were not to speak to and not to intimidate these men. On Sunday, the following day, the same message was repeated, and we were joined by the police in their panda cars who arrived as observers. The N.A.C.O.D.S. men ignored our pleas, but there were no incidents. It was spelt out quite clearly to all of us not to get involved in any incident and so fall foul of the law.

The next day, Monday, N.U.M. Lodge officials were again manning the picket line when one of our workmen, a charge-hand, turned up and started haranguing the Officials with expressions like "You bastards!", as they went in to work. With the police and the local press present, it was evident that activators were trying to stir things up, and in situations like this, tempers can easily get out of control. One of the N.A.C.O.D.S. men came back to the picket line and placed his hand on my shoulder – "Put your hand on my shoulder like this", he said, "and we'll call it intimidation and go home". What price morality? I told him to clear off, and turned around to find a free-lance journalist at my elbow waiting for some action – my comments to him were unprintable. It was to their credit that a large number of N.A.C.O.D.S. men refused to cross picket lines and never turned up for work. Knowing their terms of employment guaranteed basic pay, even if they did not turn up for work, undoubtedly swayed many waverers, and this annoyed those of their comrades who went in to work and had to do double duties to keep the pit safe. Despite one or two minor incidents the strike took its course and there was no serious disruption to our peaceful picketing. N.U.M. personnel at Ellistown, whether voting for or against strike action, stayed united and loyal to union policy. After the first week of the strike the Conservative Government decided to go to the country for public support. Parliament was dissolved and a general election called. In my opinion there was no need for this, they had a comfortable majority of around 17 in the House of Commons, but it seemed they wanted to make an issue of the miners. During the next three weeks, on the run-up to polling day, the N.U.M. executive withdrew official picket lines, and normal relations slowly began to be re-established. Though we were still on strike and turned up at the picket lines, management invited us back on to colliery premises where we were given tea and biscuits most days. The Government failed to get public support and were defeated at the ballot box.

After four weeks strike we went back to work under a Labour Government. Their first priority was to get the pits and factories back to work and to end the power cuts. The N.U.M. national executive accepted an improved wage offer and the strike was called off. Men started to come back into the pits again as other industries cut back production or went out of business. Some just could not believe the low pay which they were offered, and one family man I spoke to told me he had been better off on Social Security.

CHANGED ATTITUDES WITHIN THE UNION

After a change of Area Union Secretary in 1976, when Jack Jones took over from Frank Smith, a new productivity agreement for Leicestershire miners was negotiated by the new man, although this was against National Union policy. It was a complicated agreement, but allowed Areas to make independent decisions and enabled the introduction of production-related wage increases. However, the implementation caused a lot of bitterness and again set men against each other, mostly at the other pits. Despite some difficulties, Ellistown stayed united and this ensured that, on the four coal-faces operating, no man went home with more bonus than another. We believed in teamwork and this meant consideration for those working with you; it created a feeling of pride in the job and a collective competitive spirit to improve performance for the common good. We believed that 'good work makes good men'.

Productivity rose with the agreement, and Ellistown colliery was soon producing two and a half times the national average of 41cwt. per man-shift. But these good times were short-lived. Returning from three weeks' sick leave following an injury, I found myself in the midst of chaos. The charge-hands advised me not to go down the pit, and were calling for a wild-cat strike. Rumour had circulated that canteen ladies and secretaries employed by the Board were getting more bonuses than men working underground, and this had given rise to heated emotions. By this time I had given up my trade union activities, therefore, with other workmen, I sat in the canteen and waited for the situation to be resolved. Lodge union officials had not got a clue how to sort out the problem and seemed at a loss as how to calculate the bonus payments under dispute. After a lot of haggling the men were offered £1 per shift on top of what they had already been paid. The increase was duly accepted, and it was back to work after another unnecessary confrontation which could have been avoided with a little sensible forethought.

It may appear that I have been over-critical of the Leicestershire N.U.M. and that my comments on trade union activities are biased, but throughout my life I have believed in fair play and honesty. This may seem rather old-fashioned now, and one man's opinion, honestly held, can be quite at variance with that of his colleague working alongside him. Nevertheless, after a lifetime working in such a hostile environment where it is necessary to be always thinking about the safety and welfare of the men working with you, you develop blighted expectations of those set above you. One's early fears, hopes and ambitions have been exploited and frustrated so many times, that always the question is there about the true motives and abilities of the people who are influencing your life. Without the N.U.M. my working conditions would have been worse than those of my father, and my intention has been to point out the mistakes which occurred as I saw them and anguished over them. I have the greatest respect for men of integrity, whether they have been my mates, union officials or management, but I disdain dishonesty and incompetence.

The danger with any union is that an underlying dissatisfaction with the way things are run can cause creeping paralysis, where no one bothers to voice their opinions or offer their services because nothing would be achieved, leaving the way open for heavy handed 'political' manipulation.

What kept the local Union from becoming undemocratic were stalwarts like Alf Clarke, J.P., whose credibility, when representing men in the Industrial Tribunal courts, was unquestioned, Ernest Harding, J.P., another man of high integrity, and others with lesser positions. To make my point about these people I quote from a speech made by Alf Clark to a large contingent of his men, following his election as Snibston Lodge Delegate. Unhappily, despite the outstanding personal qualities of these leaders, there were more men within the union against them than behind them. The notes for this speech are in the possession of his widow.

Ever since an early age I have been interested in the Trade Union Movement, always I was thrilled to read of its birth, growth and development. I was brought up an ardent Methodist and the more advanced I became in Christian teaching, the more convinced I was of the moral and ethical rightness of Trade Unionism, and have made a mental resolve that should the opportunity arise I would use what little ability I possessed for the betterment of workers through the Trade Union movement. I think that the industry in which I was sent to work upon leaving school, that of coal-mining, needed more putting right than any other industry I know of, for if any type of worker has been exploited and trampled down, it is the coal-miner. Being elected as N.U.M. representative of Snibston Lodge, I realised the time had arrived for me to translate into practice those thoughts and feelings which had possessed me for years. There was one thing I was determined to do right from the start, and that was to speak the truth, both to my men and to management.

Being on the other side of the fence, so to speak, gives one a slanted view of management. However, at every stage of my working life management decisions and attitudes have played a major part in my wellbeing, finances and prospects. Such a view gave me a firm opinion of the qualities of such people who controlled my life, and I am very aware of the imbalance within the coal industry. As in all walks of life, there are the good, bad and indifferent. It seemed to me that the higher the position men held, the less they knew about mining coal. As an example of the N.C.B. taking unsuitable recruits into the industry for management training, I remember two young men from farming backgrounds, one from Somerset and the other from Dorset, who passed through my hands for face training. Both were likeable young men determined to climb the promotional ladder; but one could tell farming was in their blood, not mining. Even now, I hope they made it, and became good miners first before becoming good managers.

Coal mining in Britain is an ancient industry and working in the pits has always been a hazardous occupation. There has been traditional resentment amongst miners at the harsh treatment of the workforce by the old coal owners. Before the days of social security it was no consolation to the miner, thrown out of work with a family to feed, to know there was no demand for coal from his mine, or that severe competition had caused serious cash flow problems for the owners. Life was hard and the mining community, by reason of its deprivations and working conditions, developed social isolation which further diminished their standing in society. Coming from mining families we were brought up with this feeling that society looked down on us and would do nothing to help us break free or get better working conditions. Between the two World Wars there had been a great deal of talk about nationalisation of the coal-mining industry; the idea of the industry being owned by the people for the benefit of the people was a dream which all miners shared. The miner yearned for security, for the right to work, and the opportunity to provide a better life for himself and his family. It was a dream that was only partly to succeed.

Nationalisation created an empire which spawned new jobs at every level of administration, from National Headquarters down to Pit level, and laterally into manufacturing enterprises and service units. At Area Headquarters an army of 'stars' with their supporting administrative staff were created almost overnight, to the point where it seemed the industry must exist just to keep these people in a job. This process gradually crept into individual pits, so that when mechanisation boosted production at the coal-faces, it also boosted the army of 'stars' at pit level. But the conditions of the miner at the coal-face did not change, for new technology brought new hazards, and the miner, not the 'stars' with their fancy titles, had to 'carry the can' when things went wrong.

Sadly, this practice of buck-passing crept into the N.U.M. and in the end was partly responsible for not only destroying the coal industry, but the National Union of Mineworkers itself. Some men in our own area union had no interest in becoming miners, neither were they interested in the men they were supposed to represent; all they wanted was position and power.

MODERN TECHNOLOGY

In 1981 I was deployed on a 10ft. coal-seam, four times the height of the one we worked at New Lount Colliery. This was to be my last workplace and provided challenges equal to, and indeed greater than, any I had experienced in my life underground. The monster coal-cutting machines on this, and similar faces, were getting bigger and bigger as calls for increased productivity reached fever pitch up and down the country. Specialist manufacturers were inventing new machines employing the latest technology, and such was the geological variability of coal seams in Britain, and the demands it presented, that they were able to enter the world markets and offer mining machinery to meet any working condition. The British mining industry was now becoming second to none in the world and the Leicestershire miner was playing a big part in establishing and testing these machines. Modern technology and the age of the computer were now upon us. The coal-cutter on 61's section was unique in my experience, since no longer was a haulage chain needed for it to operate. This was a good thing, for many a man had been killed or badly injured by these dreaded chains under great tension as the cutter bit into the coal and hauled itself along the chain, and which stretched the whole length of the coal-face.

Now the machine operated along a static rack integral with the Panzer track on which it ran. We called this system the "racker-track" which worked on the same

Using lifting tackle to raise materials off a rubber-tyred trailer at Merrylees Colliery, 1964. As mechanisation brought increasingly heavy equipment into the coal mines, mechanical handling was introduced underground. In the foreground is a compact-tyred Hunslet battery tractor.

Ellistown Colliery's 61's coal-face production team, 1981. Left to right are; D.Povey (Overman), N.Ball, G.Burton, M.Woodward, T.Harding, L.Holmes and K.Ensor, with T.Lynes kneeling. Dust masks are seen around the necks of four of the men, and everyone wears a cap lamp and carries a respirator (as can be observed on the belt of the Overman). Note the difference between clean and soiled dust masks. Respirators give emergency protection against carbon monoxide in the event of a fire or explosion underground. Knee-pads were still used by most men on the coal-face. The men in the photograph partly obscure the fabricated platform on which the hydraulic powered roof support is standing. These extended supports were introduced to work at the increased heights of very thick coal seams.

principle as the Snowdon mountain railway, but with a captivating rail to prevent the machine lifting off the track. The hydraulic driving unit incorporated an electronic control system with a computer sited at the centre of the machine. Operating panels at each end of the coal-cutter enabled it to be controlled from the rear, in whichever direction it was travelling. One of the greatest novelties was that we had no manual gears to wrestle with. Instead, the machine would respond to the lightest touch on the panel and would do things never dreamed of before. This did not mean that the computer took over, but that it caused the machine to do exactly what you directed it to do. Operators had to have a great deal of face experience, especially in regulating and controlling the roof and floor.

After about nine months of trials, and despite the potential of these machines, senior management were pressing the men to repeat mistakes made 20 years earlier at the introduction of mechanisation. These were mainly in roof and floor control, but this time on a much larger scale. So it was no surprise to us old hands when production eventually came to a standstill.

Out of the 10ft. coal-seam, over 2ft. of coal was being left in the floor; this meant that the machine was cutting in the stone roof. When the situation was eventually rectified, the coal-cutting team was split up and two teams formed. I was asked by the face production Overman, Don Povey, to go on to driving the machine. He was a practical and knowledgeable young man, with mining in his blood, who was overridden many times by ignorant or jealous supervisors. Senior officials talked about economics, techniques and motivation but these terms were so much hot air when it came to put them into practice. Where co-operation and trust should have existed between the two teams a wedge was driven; production suffered and any suggestions made by the experienced men on the job were frowned upon and ignored. By now our team were determined to put our own theories to the test. We had a meeting to sort out how best we could seek vindication and motivate ourselves to make our ideas work. It was thought the best way would be by turning more coal than the other team, and I was elected to lead our team. By tightening up our teamwork and reducing machine standing time, by doing preparation work at both ends of the coal-face at the same time as the machine was stood down, our efficiency was considerably improved. During the first week we produced three times the amount of coal previously achieved and increased our bonuses on the section from £6 to £14 per shift. This showed what the machine could really do, and had more than fulfilled the expectations of the manufacturer. Prospective purchasers came from all over the world – U.S.A., South Africa, Australia and the Shell oil company – to see the machine in action and talk to the men who operated it. We believed some financial reward would be forthcoming in recognition of our enthusiastic endeavours as salesmen, but none came our way!

ABNORMAL WORKING CONDITIONS

The next episode of my working life was yet another affront to common sense and a lesson in union duplicity. The coal seam we were working on had a stone band eight to ten inches thick running through the middle. In the old days of hand filling this stone would have been separated as the coal was loaded, but on a shearer face (cut by machine) the machine grinds its way through coal and stone alike. Not only does the presence of stone in the coal have an adverse effect on its quality, but stone-dust is the main cause of pneumoconiosis and therefore a serious health hazard. The modern coal preparation plant is able to remove the larger stone pieces by washing the coal, and power station smalls -which are not washed- can be blended with high grade slack to reduce its ash content. Quality of the mined coal was therefore sacrificed in the interests of production, leaving the operational health hazard unaddressed. Somewhere along the line, management was persuaded into trying out the Bretby large-pick coal-cutting discs. Each was 2m in diameter and had fewer but bigger picks, and replaced two 1.5m discs, one of which cut under and the other over the stone band. This change was presumably based on the assumption that more large lumps would be produced, but the problem was considerably aggravated as the original discs were just right to cut the coal without touching the stone band.

Now, the new discs ground into the stone band so that it became practically impossible to see your hand in front of you, let alone breathe. We wondered by now if anyone in management had any practical experience at all. H.M. Inspector of Mines could and should have closed the section down, for the dust levels in the vicinity of the shearer were way above the legal limits. To compound our misery, water was also seeping in through the strata, making very wet conditions on the face. So, once again I found myself knocking on the manager's door, asking for extra payment for men working in these abnormal conditions. After lengthy discussions it was agreed that all men on the section would receive an extra £2 a day and that anyone else, such as fitters and electricians, required to work on the face would also receive this payment. The agreement was to last for six weeks, during which time it was expected that we would have re-established normal working conditions. All was to go well for four weeks then we found ourselves in the midst of a wild-cat strike.

UNION INTERFERENCE

As part of routine procedures at the mine, union officials – one each from the National Union of Mineworkers, National Association of Colliery Overmen and Deputies, and Power Group – inspected the section. Their resulting report stated that, in their opinion, working conditions did not warrant the extra payment we were getting. The absurdity of this assertion was emphasised by the fact that one of the Union men pushed the stop button on the machine because they could not see for dust. Management were only too ready to accept their report and we heard that the extra money was to be stopped. As charge-hand it was my duty to try to sort this crisis out. My proposal was to see the manager next day, but on a show of hands the team voted to walk off the job until the matter was settled. Before walking out with them, I was called to the telephone by the manager and asked to get the men back to work. I had to tell him that the matter was now out of my hands as a vote had been taken and the men would stay out until the agreement was reinstated. We all went home disgusted by events, but every-one reported for work next day.

In the canteen, other charge-hands and workmen pledged their support. They were asked to go to work and not inflame the situation, for if common sense prevailed the problem could easily be resolved. Alas, there was a marked absence of common sense and the situation looked like getting out of hand. We were told that if we would go down the pit, the manager and union men would negotiate the dispute. Our reply was that if the union men hadn't interfered in the first place no one would be in this situation, and we now had no confidence in them. However, after four hours of hard discussions, also involving two other team members, the manager agreed to honour the original agreement; so it was back to work and business as usual with a lesson learned. Union officials had special privileges and some did not have to go down the pit and work like we did. They were supposed to represent the interests of the men producing the coal that paid their wages, but instead were prepared to be used by management. Where now were the honest men of high integrity?

THE LAST STRAW

The final episode which convinced me it was time to hang up my pit boots came again from an absurd situation; one in which management fell short of their responsibilities and face workers were once more placed in a 'no win' situation. Colliery output targets, and our own bonus payments, depended on the machines being kept running, often in very difficult conditions. The face team had to be masters of improvisation to coax and cajole the heavy unwieldy machinery over and around the many geological irregularities that presented themselves during a working shift. 'Keep the face turning', but for your own safety keep your eyes and ears open and use your common sense – that was our motto. On this particular day we were struggling a bit, but the coal was coming away from the face nicely and, as charge-hand, I was fully occupied with matters of the moment when I received a message that H.M. Inspector of Mines wanted to see me down the coal-face. He wanted to know why the chock shields (roof supports) had not been extended right forward to support the front of the 11ft. high face, since coal breaking away on its own was very dangerous. As the shearer progressed down the face it left an unsupported section of coal-face behind it and the chockers (operators of powered supports) then had to extend the shields on the powered supports after the Panzer was pushed over and the chocks advanced. The Inspector was standing with the team member, whose job it was to operate the chocks, but would not accept his explanation. As usual, the Inspector was escorted by the Undermanager and Deputy, but both remained silent when asked why the man had been allowed to disobey the rules, although they knew the reasons very well.

The face installation had been designed and installed for a level floor, but as the face advanced it developed a temporary downhill gradient of 1 in 6 dipping towards the coal-face, which meant the chock side of the Panzer being four inches higher than the face side. When the hydraulic shield-rams were fully extended they could cut through the electric power cable, so stopping production for the day. This was not a new problem; everyone knew about it and just left us to get on with the job of cutting coal. There were Rules. The Manager's Support Rules were posted and said the shields had to be extended right up to the face. These were standard rules which were generally accepted and applied in normal working conditions. Management knew that to obey this rule to the letter would bring the coal-face to a permanent standstill and, instead of altering the Rule had turned a blind eye to the practice, thus throwing the responsibility on to the face team if anything had gone wrong. Appealing again to the officials for support, we were met by the same silence and were obliged to obey the Inspector. When, as expected, the inevitable happened I looked for the Inspector but he had fled. Chasing after him to explain the results of his actions, I got no-where. He too remained silent and seemed to disassociate himself from the whole incident. We were left to clear up the mess and carry on as before.

REDUNDANCY, 1982

Since starting work in 1937 at Snibston colliery, my whole mining career has been spent underground. In that time tremendous changes have taken place in the industry, and continue to do so. I have seen and been involved in the implementation of new ideas which, in less than 50 years, have changed coal mining practice beyond the wildest dreams of pre-war miners. A collier of the 1930s would have been quite 'at home' in the coal pits of the 1830s, and indeed those of a hundred years earlier; but the rate of progress of modern technology and the application of scientific principles is now such that it needs young men to sustain the pace. So, in 1982, six months before my sixtieth birthday, I received a letter on my lamp informing me the National Coal Board no longer required my services, and that I was to be made redundant in August. I received a certificate thanking me for "37 years" loyal efficient service to the industry and country. It was no surprise they could not even get my 45-year service record correct!

Leicestershire coal miners have always shown loyalty to their job and to their country, but this loyalty has been consistently taken for granted and exploited. Whether it was the private owner, nationalised management, union officials or government, the ordinary working miner's integrity has been traditionally abused. Despite all the technological changes, the one thing that does not seem to change is human nature! And so I was glad that my working life was over and relieved to be out of the daily hassle. In the pit canteen my mates presented me with a silver beer tankard and a Parker pen. With the tankard I have, on numerous occasions, toasted the health of my many friends, and with the pen I have written these mining memoirs as a tribute to the humble miner, now only a memory in the once-great Leicestershire coalfield.

Ostlers and Pit-ponies, at Whitwick Colliery, late 1960s. "Peter" and the rest of Whitwick pit-ponies are brought to the surface after working their last shift underground. This photograph shows ostlers Sammy Clamp and Cyril Tilsley with two of their charges on Whitwick Colliery surface after their ride up the shaft. Mechanisation in the coal mines had made both ponies and ostlers redundant.

Epilogue

Now, like "Jasper" and the rest of the pit ponies years earlier, it was my turn to be put out to grass, so to speak. My first experience was like a bird being released from a cage with all the freedom it entailed; for like generations of miners before me, our confining cage had been the heading, the coal-face and the travelling roads below ground.

The area north of Coalville, with Bardon Hill rising over nine hundred feet above sea level, is without doubt one of the most beautiful parts of Leicestershire, and I was determined to adjust the new life to claim my true heritage, walking the footpaths as I did when a boy. During my working life I have had to rise early and this habit was one of the most difficult things to break; it was therefore on many an early morning that I found myself wandering the lanes, fields and woods of Charnwood Forest. To find yourself alone in the calm of a wood after an autumn night-frost, when the wind suddenly stirs in fitful gusts and the multi-coloured leaves fall like so many snowflakes, is one of the wonders of nature which had been denied me until now. The hares, rabbits, foxes, squirrels, the wild life on the ponds, were all part of this new life. Sun, wind, rain, even snow did not deter me from this new-found freedom; the sound of the early morning Monastery bell which called the monks to prayer, also called me home for breakfast. The freedom was mine to stay, lingering awhile on the rocks above our town to see commuters hurrying to work and hear the playful sound of children in the schools just below. It seems like yesterday that I rejoiced amid all this beauty, and sang the well known hymn line, 'till we have built Jerusalem in England's green and pleasant land'. What joy can be ours when our hearts are at peace.

The opinions expressed in these memoirs are personal ones and the experiences only a small part of what Leicestershire miners shared together. No doubt other stories will be told in the future, for many have travelled the same road and remember tragedies, heartache, disappointment and elation. They remember those who did not survive to retirement age, those with scars and injuries which bear testimony to the work they did, and yet others, broken in health by the conditions under which they worked. Like me, they also remember the friends they made and the close bond of comradeship which was established between groups of men thrown together in difficult circumstances. The Leicestershire coalfield is no more, but memories will linger on. We have been part of a local history covering a thousand years, of a national industry still struggling for survival. Whatever the future holds in store, we are proud to have been part of the past.